Environment

by James Everest

Aladdin Paperbacks

Text copyright © 1995 by Aladdin Paperbacks
Photographs and logo copyright © 1995 by National Broadcasting
Company, Inc. *Name Your Adventure*™ is a trademark of National
Broadcasting Company, Inc. Used under license.
All rights reserved, including the right of reproduction in whole
or in part in any form
Aladdin Paperbacks
An imprint of Simon and Schuster
Children's Publishing Division
1230 Avenue of the Americas
New York, NY 10020
Manufactured in the United States of America
10 9 8 7 6 5 4 3 2 1
Designed by Chani Yammer
Library of Congress Cataloging-in-Publication Data
Everest, James.
Name your adventure. Environment / by James Everest. — 1st Aladdin
Paperbacks ed.
p.   cm.
ISBN 0-02-045475-9
1. Environmental sciences—Juvenile literature. 2. Natural history—
Juvenile literature. 3. Name your adventure (Television program)—
Juvenile literature. [1. Environmental sciences. 2. Natural history.
3. Name your adventure (Television program)] I. Name your adventure
(Television program) II. Title.
GE115.E84 1995
363.7—dc20   94-38817

To environmental adventurers everywhere

CONTENTS

Environmental Mania!	8
Oceanography—Under the Sea	11
Fossils—Digging Up More Than Bones	34
Recycling—Putting Natural Resources to Work	58
Rain Forests—Life under the Canopy	78
Dolphins—Encounter of the Closest Kind	102
Name *Your* Adventure	126

Environmental Mania!

Can't get enough of Mario Lopez as Slater on *Saved by the Bell*? Then how about Mario as an environmental crusader on *Name Your Adventure*? Together with cohost Jordan Brady, Mario and the *Name Your Adventure* crew take lucky viewers around the world each week in search of adventure and fantasy. If you can dream it, they just might make it happen.

In this book, we'll climb a mountain of garbage waiting to be recycled. We'll hunt for fossil clues to our planet's history. We'll check out the towering Sitka spruce and the northern spotted owl controversy in America's very own rain forest, go to Hawaii with Mario and swim with the dolphins at Dolphin Quest, and even dive into the crystal clear waters of the Florida Keys.

Garbage may not sound so adventurous, but garbage and recycling are real passions for Bahar Soomekh. Her idea of adventure was wading through a mountain of recyclable plastic at an actual recycling center.

Paleontologist-in-training Vivek Varughese wanted to find out about some *really* old leftovers. When he got to see a baby mammoth being excavated firsthand, he discovered that fossils aren't just bones—they're like a history lesson without the teacher. And they're easier to find than you might expect. Read on for some tips for finding fossils in your own backyard!

Speaking of backyards, most of us don't have to walk very far from our backyard to visit a forest, but seventeen-year-old Elise Kovar took off for Oregon to find out what we can do to save the last American rain forests. Unfortunately, they are disappearing at an alarming rate, and taking the plants and animals that make their home there with them. But saving them is easier than you might think.

We'll leave behind the animals of the rain forest to go and swim with the dolphins. Renee Gragnano got her chance to find out what's involved in training dolphins and what it takes to have a career as a marine mammal trainer when she visited Dolphin Quest with Mario. Come along for the ride—you don't even have to get wet!

You could hardly stay dry if you wanted to learn about the ocean. Rick Sage literally went head over heels into the Florida Keys to explore the health of two different coral reefs. He even had the opportunity to go where no teenager has ever gone before—just keep reading to find out where.

ENVIRONMENT

So thanks, Mario and Jordan, for being our tour guides on all these wonderful adventures and helping us explore so many interesting topics!

Oceanography— Under the Sea

Feel like setting sail for the turquoise waters of the Florida Keys? Rick Sage did, and *Name Your Adventure* was only too happy to oblige. Rick and Jordan boarded the research vessel *Agassiz* to check on the health of a couple of coral reefs down in the Keys—and to catch a few rays along the way!

To make sure he would be picked to set sail, Rick sent in not one, but two videos! "The reason I want to be on *Name Your Adventure*," Rick stated on his videotape, "is because I've always loved the water." Rick would really love to be a marine biologist because he wants to help people learn about animals and plants and corals and, he hopes, make them realize how important they are.

To help reach his goal, Rick took a scuba course to become a certified diver. In fact, his entire family is certified. Rick, his mother, his father, and his older brother, Brian, all go diving together. Ever since he got certified two years ago, Rick spends as much time in the water as possible. And *Name Your Adventure* gave him the per-

ENVIRONMENT

Fish You'll Find in a Coral Reef

Exactly what types of fish and sea creatures should you look for when exploring a coral reef? There are hundreds of species, but here are a few common ones.

On the bottom of the reef floor you'll find sponges, starfish, hermit crabs, brain corals, feather dusters, sea urchins, and staghorn corals.

A bit farther up swim the queen angelfish, four-eyed butterfly fish, fan coral, hawksbill sea turtle, and a little critter known as the porcupine puffer.

On top of the coral reef is the majestic queen triggerfish, the elkhorn coral, and the appropriately named lookdown fish!

fect opportunity to jump right in and put his scuba certification to good use!

Rick's first stop: the Molasses Reef. Located in the National Marine Sanctuary in the Florida Keys, it is the only living coral reef in the United States, and the third largest reef in the world. It may be just a country cousin compared to Australia's Great Barrier Reef, but it's still a living, breathing ecosystem—and a spectacular place to scuba dive.

Rick and Jordan strapped on their scuba gear with Paige Gill, the education director at the National Marine Sanctuary. Paige has Rick's ultimate dream job; she's a marine biologist who helps people learn about the amazing reef environment. With over a million divers visiting the Molasses Reef each year, she has plenty of opportunities to educate folks about the importance of this incredibly beautiful site. And Rick and Jordan got a chance to see what makes it so worthy of protection.

Reefs are made up of billions of tiny sea creatures called coral. Reef-building coral can survive only where the water temperature stays above seventy degrees Fahrenheit. Each coral releases a hard covering, and it's this hard covering that forms the coral reef. The neon-bright pieces of coral you see for sale in souvenir shops aren't the live animals, but the dead exoskeletons left behind by millions of tiny coral creatures.

When Paige and Rick checked out Molasses Reef, they wore Augie masks so they could talk back and forth about their underwater discoveries. These special diving masks have actual microphones in the front. These microphones pick up divers' voices, allowing them to communicate (with other divers who are wearing the masks) via earphones in the sides. (Poor Jordan had to rely on sign language.)

As the three made their way through the crystal clear water to the coral reef, they were met by a variety of brightly colored fish. Rick was amazed when he came across a huge piece of brain coral—which does look eerily like a real live brain.

Pass the Salt, Please

You can't swim in the ocean without noticing how salty it is. That's because ocean water has a high percentage of salts (or salinity), like sodium, magnesium, chloride, and other ions, present in it. Three-quarters of the salt in the ocean is sodium chloride—the same stuff we use as common table salt.

The oceans are the end of the hydrologic cycle. Rain and snow carry all types of minerals—the things that make the water salty—into the water. There is salt in river water, but it's carried to the ocean where it stays for a very long period of time. Water evaporates into the atmosphere, then falls back to the land as rain, eroding more rock and carrying more ions to the sea. But those ions don't evaporate. Over time, they accumulate, along with sodium chloride, and make the ocean more and more salty. Right now there is enough salt in the ocean to cover the land with a layer five hundred feet thick.

ENVIRONMENT

"What can we learn by studying coral reefs?" Jordan asked Paige when they returned to the deck of the *Agassiz*. What he found out was that a coral reef is just as valuable an ecosystem as a tropical rain forest. A healthy coral reef offers some of the same benefits, such as food from the fish that swim there, shelter from hurricanes and storms, and drugs that can reverse the effects of heart disease, speed the healing of stomach ulcers, and even lower blood pressure.

The National Marine Sanctuary won't let just anyone come in and drop anchor at Molasses Reef. They take special precautions to make sure that the coral reef stays happy and healthy. For example, the "beach balls" that Jordan noticed right away are actually buoys—floating objects that mark where permanent anchors are placed for boats to hook up to. This way the coral won't get damaged by lots of sailors throwing anchors in the water.

Unfortunately, there was a lot more than anchor damage to worry about at the second coral reef Rick, Jordan, and Paige visited. It had no healthy corals and hardly any fish. And the fish that were there could barely be seen through the murky water.

To find out exactly why coral reefs get "sick" like this, Rick hooked up with Dr. Steve Miller, the science director of the National Undersea Re-search Center, at his lab on a floating barge. According to Paige and Steve, the runoff from gas and fertilizers used on land seems to be the main culprit. When these pollutants enter the water, they encourage the growth of algae—that's seaweed to us landlubbers! Too much algae can "cloud out" the coral so that it can't get enough sunlight. And without enough sunlight, a reef hasn't got a chance.

To better understand the difference between a healthy coral reef and a sick one, Rick visited the *Aquarius*, an underwater research facility in the Florida Keys. People actually live and work in the *Aquarius* (which looks like a giant metal bubble at the bottom of the sea) for periods of up to ten days, addressing issues

ENVIRONMENT

related to the health and status of the coral reefs in the Florida Keys.

Rick got to find out firsthand what the *Aquarius* (pictured above) was all about. In fact, Rick was the first teenager to ever visit the *Aquarius*! Here oceanographers from all over the world study different factors, such as diminished water quality, to see how they affect the coral reef. They take water samples and measure the amounts of ammonium nitrate, phosphate, and other chemicals in the water. In the Florida Keys, there's great

Oceanography

concern that damaging amounts of nutrients, particularly nitrogen and phosphorus, are entering the water from development activities and sewage.

Surprisingly, though, Dr. Miller says that really very little is known about the health of the reefs in the Florida Keys. Scientists, in fact, are still trying to understand the difference between the two reefs that Rick visited during his adventure and to identify all the factors that affect their health.

Rick got to take part in this research. He and Steve

Only One Ocean

A ONE-SECOND QUIZ

How many oceans exist on earth? If you said anything but one, you're technically wrong! "The ocean" refers to that one humongous body of salt water that covers 70 percent of the earth's surface. Check out a globe and you'll see that it's all connected: The ocean is actually one body of water. Which means that the continents we live on are simply large islands set in the ocean! Still, it's awfully inconvenient to refer to it that way—so we've divided the ocean into four oceans. Alphabetically, they are . . .

1. The Arctic Ocean, which surrounds the North Pole. It is the smallest of the four, covering an area of 5,427,000 square miles.

2. The Atlantic Ocean, which borders the East Coast of the United States, is the second largest at 31,744,000 square miles.

3. The Indian Ocean is situated east of Africa. At 28,371,000 square miles, it is smaller than the Atlantic and Pacific.

4. The Pacific Ocean, which laps onto the California, Oregon, and Washington coastline, is the granddaddy of them all, at a whopping 63,855,000 square miles.

collected water samples with a special two-lidded specimen bottle. By sealing water tightly inside the bottle, there's little chance that it will get contaminated when transported from where it was collected to where it will be analyzed by oceanographers.

Rick and Jordan met a lot of oceanographers during their underwater adventure, but what do oceanographers do when they're not giving tours to teens? Basically, oceanographers study large bodies of water: oceans, seas, and the great lakes of the world. They may also be interested in what goes on in smaller areas of water like bays, gulfs, and lagoons.

Of course, that definition's about as broad as an ocean itself. So let's break it down into four sub-specialties that get a lot more specific.

MARINE LIFE MANIA!

The first group, *biological oceanographers*, study the diversity of marine life in the oceans to see how it develops over time. They look at plants and animals so small they can only be seen with a microscope, all the way up to the blue whale, the largest animal ever to exist.

A biological oceanographer's job includes identifying the species found in a particular body of water. Discovering new species and their relationships to others is always an exciting possibility. And because life on earth evolved from the ocean, biological oceanographers may also study life histories.

The scientists that Rick and Jordan met on *Name Your Adventure* were all biological oceanographers. Their main concern was the ecology of the marine community—the way the different organisms interact within the coral reefs. How does the health of the reef affect the fish that live there? What do the fish eat and what eats them in turn? "Interconnection" and "interdependence" are the bread and butter of a biological oceanographer's job.

Other biological oceanographers take what we know about marine communities and look at the impact on humans. After all, much of the world's food supply comes from oceans. In coastal populations, especially in Asian countries, the ocean provides most of the protein in people's diets. How can we continue to take certain types of marine life like seaweed, oysters, clams, cod, or salmon, and still have a food resource that is going to last? If that kind of question intrigues you, then biological oceanography might just be your thing.

WHY IS THE SEA SALTY?

If you'd rather find out what makes the sea salty, maybe you should consider *chemical oceanography*. Chemical oceanographers study the various chemicals in the oceans, where these chemicals come from, and how they are distributed.

Chemical oceanographers also study how various elements, such as carbon, cycle—or circulate—throughout the ocean. One problem that a chemical oceanographer might work on is how the greenhouse effect impacts on our oceans. Carbon dioxide goes from the atmosphere into the water and then from the water back into the atmosphere. Since carbon dioxide is utilized by plants on land and in the water, a chemical oceanographer could study how plants underwater use carbon dioxide and how this process differs from plants on land.

LET'S GET PHYSICAL!

If you're a body boarder who's always dreaming of the perfect wave, then *physical oceanography* could be the career for you. Just like you, physical oceanographers spend most of their time thinking about waves—and tides and currents and other ways that water moves. After all, the wet stuff doesn't just sit there!

Here's a crash course in Currents 101: Wind and the earth's rotation make the water swirl around, forming currents. Physical oceanographers figure out how currents flow, how they change, and how fast they move.

ENVIRONMENT

These could be small, local currents or huge patterns like the California Current or the Gulf Stream.

The Gulf Stream is actually a large river within the Atlantic Ocean that carries warm water north to Canada, then swings up to the Arctic Circle and curves back down to England. At its narrowest, it's two to three miles across; at its widest, maybe ten times that. The water within the current actually has a different temperature and salt content than the water that flows around it.

Current shmurrent, you say? What's the big deal about a dumb bunch of water? Well, currents ultimately affect the health and population of marine life. In the long run, that can mean the difference between whether you get tuna fish or peanut butter for lunch!

Currents can also influence weather patterns up to thousands of miles away. Maybe you've heard of the current called El Niño that flows in the Pacific near the equator. Some years, it's incredibly strong; other years, it's barely there at all. Its strength influences how much moisture evaporates from the Pacific Ocean—and how much it's going to rain down on the land. Because the wind patterns in our part of the world move from west to east, farmers as far away as Iowa can be affected by what this one distant current pattern is up to!

You say that waves and currents just don't grab

Look Out! Big Waves in the Harbor!

Tidal waves are the most destructive types of waves. Fortunately, they are pretty rare. Actually, you may be surprised to learn that tidal waves aren't even caused by the tides. Called "tsunamis" (soo-NAH-meez), a Japanese word for "large waves in harbor," they are caused by earthquakes, volcanic eruptions, or underwater avalanches. These events cause shock waves to travel outward across the ocean, widening as they go. You can see the same rippling effect if you drop a pebble in a pail of water. In deep water, these waves can travel as fast as six hundred miles per hour. At that speed, a tsunami can destroy an ocean city in minutes.

The greatest reported tidal waves occurred after the explosion of a volcanic island in the South Pacific named Krakatau, in 1883. The explosion was so violent that it could be heard three thousand miles away. (That would be like standing in New York City and hearing something that happened in San Francisco!) As the island collapsed, a wave more than 120 feet high smashed into nearby islands and killed thousands of people, sank ships, and scattered debris. It even picked up one huge ship and carried it two miles inland.

ENVIRONMENT

you? Then how about self-exploding squids? Not a pretty thought, but it's something that physical oceanographers also have to consider when they're studying water pressure.

Pressure underwater increases with depth. That's why you feel your ears clog up when you dive deep into a pool. The pressure within your body is less than the pressure in the water. If you hold your nose and blow, you can equalize the pressure and your ears unclog in a second or two. But equalizing pressure gets trickier the deeper you go because water pressure increases about 15 pounds per square inch for every 30 feet of depth.

Rick went 65 feet under to the *Aquarius*. That equals out to be a little over 30 pounds of pressure per square inch. At 100 feet underwater, the pressure's about 50 pounds per square inch. Jordan and Rick really had to take their time when diving and resurfacing to allow the pressure to equalize comfortably.

What's all this got to do with splattering squid guts? Well, some pretty amazing creatures live up to seven miles below the surface of the ocean. One of them happens to be a colossal species of squid. Because the pressure at this depth is eight tons per square inch, if these animals were suddenly brought up to the surface, they'd explode! Their body pressure wouldn't get a chance to equalize to the new, lower level. Scientists have found

Oceans in Motion

Waves of Info You Didn't Know!

1. Earth is the only planet in the solar system with a vast ocean of water. By comparison, Mercury and Venus are bone dry; Mars is ice. Scientists believe that this is why Earth is probably the only life-bearing planet.

2. Life itself actually began in the ocean, approximately 3.5 billion years ago.

3. Unlike land temperatures, ocean temperatures don't change very much with the seasons. The average ocean temperature is thirty-eight degrees Fahrenheit, year-round.

4. Half the people in the United States live within ten miles of the ocean.

5. Water, water everywhere: 70 percent of our earth is covered with water.

6. The ocean holds 97 percent of the world's water, but it's undrinkable. Three percent of the earth's water is freshwater, but since 2 percent of that is locked in glaciers and the polar ice cap, only 1 percent is available for us to drink.

7. In many cities in poor nations, there is not enough clean water for drinking and bathing. Many people living in these cities get diseases from polluted water.

8. The average price for water in North America is $1.27 for one thousand gallons. One penny buys 126 eight-ounce glasses of water.

ENVIRONMENT

remains of these creatures in the stomachs of whales and would love to get a chance to study them in the wild—but they just can't take the pressure!

WHO SAYS THE OCEAN FLOOR IS FLAT?

If you're the kind of person who always gets in over your head, you might want to check out the fourth specialty: *geological oceanography*. Geological oceanographers are the folks who study the ocean floor. They don't always do their work underwater, but often have to rely on sound instead. By sending sound waves down to the bottom of the ocean and measuring how quickly they bounce back, oceanographers can tell how close or far away the ocean floor is. This kind of echo sounding helped oceanographers discover that the ocean floor is even bumpier than the dry land that we live on!

In fact, the tallest mountain in the world isn't in the Himalayas, it's in the middle of the Pacific Ocean! If you've ever seen Mount Kiluaa off the coast of Hawaii, then you've been looking at its peak. It starts out on the ocean floor and rises two thousand feet above the water's surface.

The deepest point in the ocean is also located in the Pacific Ocean. It's a deep crack—or trench—in the ocean floor. Called the Mariana Trench, it goes seven miles down. That's double the depth of the Grand Canyon!

Geological oceanographers don't just measure depths. They also study the sediment that covers the ocean floor. Sediment is made up of solid materials, like sand, mud, and gravel, that have settled on the bottom, as well as the remains of any organisms that have lived in the water: fish bones, rotting algae, and, yes, squid guts. Just like fossils, these sediments record the history of a particular body of water.

A geological oceanographer working alone may go out a couple of miles from shore and study the sediments he or she finds there. His or her work would include what goes on in the sediment and how the animals there—clams, worms, and lobsters—interact with it.

That type of research is important because every pollutant that's introduced into a body of water attaches to a sediment. The sediments have charged surfaces, like magnets, that attract pollutants. Once attached, the sediment and the pollutant settle to the floor. If everything were equal, the pollutants would pile up and get buried, but they don't. That's because the animals that live in the sediment churn them around, either bringing old pollutants back to the surface or diluting new pollutants by mixing them with older, cleaner sediments.

Who's Pollutin' Our Oceans? (Duh, We Are!)

So you think it's the giant tankers and their accidental oil spills that are primarily responsible for polluting the oceans? The truth is, that accounts for only 12 percent of the mess. The other 88 percent is no accident: It's because we use the ocean as one giant dumping ground!

Nonpoint source pollution—a new term to learn—means that when we trash our stash in the usual way, it often finds its way into local waterways. Many things we do, like dumping motor oil into streams or catch basins, overusing fertilizers and pesticides, and carelessly handling household chemicals and animal waste, all cause these pollutants to end up in the ocean.

Whenever it rains, the flow of rainwater picks up pollutants from streets, parking lots, lawns, and gardens. The polluted water either runs off directly into nearby streams or other waterways, or flows into storm drains and is carried through underground pipes into local waterways. Eventually, it ends up in the ocean.

We know that water evaporates into the air and rains back down to the earth. Keeping our water clean and using it wisely will help make sure we have safe water in the future.

Oceanography

The oldest sediment on the ocean floor is only 50 to 60 million years old, because ocean floors aren't permanent. Oceanographers believe that the rock deep beneath the oceans and continents is so hot that it actually flows! As this rock slowly moves, it pulls the ocean floor apart and shifts the continents around—usually so slowly that it's imperceptible, but sometimes so suddenly that we feel it as an earthquake. This spreading of the ocean floor and the movement of the continents is called the continental drift theory.

Geological oceanographers' research has also helped to prove that our current six continents were at one time a single giant land mass. Known as Pangaea, it was set in the middle of one enormous ocean. As the plates of the earth's crust slowly drifted away from each other, fractures appeared in this ancient megacontinent. Antarctica swung southward. India moved northward and crashed into Asia, forming the Himalayas at impact. North America drifted away from Europe, and South America broke off from Africa. Look at South America and Africa on a map and you'll see that they sort of fit together like two pieces of a jigsaw puzzle.

Just for Fun: Cut the shapes of each continent out of paper and try to fit them all together into one large piece. Then slide them slowly apart until they are in their

ENVIRONMENT

current positions on a map of today's world. This will give you an idea of how the six continents were created.

GOING WHERE NO MAN—OR TEENAGER—HAS GONE BEFORE

Oceanography is a relatively new science. In fact, the first oceanographic expedition was mounted only a little over a century ago when the *Challenger*, the first ship equipped for ocean exploration, set sail from England in 1872 for a three-and-a-half-year cruise. These were the earliest investigations of the physics, chemistry, geology, and biology of the world's oceans, and included mapping features of the ocean floor, measuring properties of seawater, and collecting organisms that were swimming and floating in the sea.

Oceanography took huge strides forward during World War II. The United States government was concerned about submarine warfare, weather conditions for ships on the ocean, and how the strength of certain currents would affect landing

What Do You Call an Ocean Explorer?

An aquanaut! Just like an astronaut, an aquanaut is a highly trained expert who explores our oceans and seas, hoping to gather information helpful to our planet and our way of life.

troops on beaches. Government-hired oceanographers did in-depth studies to find answers to these and many other questions.

Today, only a few large institutions, mostly government supported, conduct oceanographic research. That's because it's mega-expensive to run ocean research vessels—anywhere between ten thousand and twenty thousand dollars a day! Why's the bill so high for a simple day on the water? Because all the high-tech research equipment they carry—everything from radar and echo sounders to submersibles—carries a pretty hefty price tag. If you're hoping to be an independent oceanographer, you'd better start saving your allowance now!

Actually, it's pretty unusual to work as an "independent" oceanographer. Most deep-sea research is conducted by scientific parties. No, that doesn't mean that they get to stay up late listening to loud music—just that their ship will probably carry thirty to fifty, or even more, people, including all four types of oceanographers.

By working together and sharing their knowledge, they can create a much fuller picture of life in our oceans than if they all worked separately. The geological oceanographers will collect data and samples from the ocean floor. The biological oceanographers will cast nets

ENVIRONMENT

to collect everything from plankton to giant kelp. The chemical oceanographers will draw water samples. The physical oceanographers will drop sensors over the side to measure temperature, salinity, and pressure.

Because oceanographic excursions usually stay at sea for several months at a time, the research vessel also carries a crew who will run the equipment and look after the scientists. So while the oceanographers are busy researching, the navigator, the captain, and even the cook are working, too. After all, even oceanographers have to eat!

What can you do if you're interested in oceanography, but you live someplace landlocked like Kansas? Luckily, you don't need to live near an ocean to get started. Many of the same principles of marine ecology and water dynamics apply to inland waters as well as oceans. You might want to find out why a local river bends in certain areas and not in others. Does it flow faster along one bank than the other? Is it shallow or deep? What types of plants and animals make it their habitat? These are similar to questions you might ask if you were studying an ocean environment, and they require the exact same research skills of observation, collection, and documentation.

If you're like Rick and dreaming about oceanography, what should you do to get ready? Stay awake in chemistry class, for one thing, suggests Dr. Miller. And take as much math as you can handle. Oceanography is really just physics (lots of math there) and chemistry applied to particular marine systems. The actual marine biology courses come later—sort of like the "icing on the cake."

If you're into science, like the outdoors, and—oh yeah—like to swim, then you're on the right track to becoming an oceanographer. And after completing his adventure, Rick is already well on his way. He knows a lot more about the underwater world. "I'm more knowledgeable about the reefs and what it takes for all this stuff to live down there," Rick said.

To help Rick remember his adventure, Steve gave him a special emblem from the National Undersea Research Center. "You handled yourself extremely well in the water and in the habitat," Steve told Rick, and he wished him the best of luck with his dreams.

"Since I was the first teenager down there," Rick said, "if you could put that on a scale of excitement from one to ten, I'd say that was an eleven."

We'd have to agree!

Fossils—Digging Up More Than Bones

Most American landfills are actually landfulls, but who could have imagined that the Madera County, California, landfill would be full of prehistoric leftovers! Jordan and amateur paleontologist Vivek Varughese went "down in the dumps" to check out some fresh fossil finds that no one even knew about before the county bulldozers rolled in.

Vivek first checked out prehistoric animals in science class when he learned about dinosaurs. From there, he went to the library and got out as many books as he could about dinosaurs. Yes, it's hard to believe—even Jordan was amazed—but Vivek actually went to the library on his own!

The main reason for Vivek's interest in prehistoric animals and their fossil remains comes from the fact that nobody has ever actually seen them before. Plus, some of these animals were so big—and yet they all evolved into the creatures that are on the earth today.

THEM BONES, THEM BONES, THEM DRY BONES

So what is a fossil, anyway? Maybe you've called your parents or a teacher "fossils" because you think they're ancient—well, you're on the right track, because all fossils are old. In fact, fossils are any remains of animals or plants that lived long ago. Most living things don't become fossilized after death because their remains are usually eaten by animals or destroyed by weather. But sometimes when a plant or animal dies, it falls into the water or sinks into the mud. Next stop: Fossil City!

CREATION OF A FOSSIL

Let's journey back millions of years ago and imagine how a fossil was created. We'll use the mighty Brachiosaurus. He was the heaviest animal to ever live on land. He weighed eighty-five tons—that's as much as fifteen elephants! You definitely wouldn't want him stepping on your foot.

Maybe our Brachiosaurus finished his days beside a calm pond, eating the leaves from a nearby tree. In the end, he could have either died in the water, or close enough to fall into the pond. Because of his extreme weight, the Brachiosaurus's remains quickly sank to the bottom and were buried and protected by mud.

Now as long as the Brachiosaurus is not disturbed or washed up, he stands a good chance of becoming fossilized. As the sand and mud harden and change to rock, the remains are locked inside. Minerals seep in and petrify them over time.

Mineral-rich remains like teeth, bone, or shell fossilize easily. Soft tissue like muscles and skin isn't quite as likely to fossilize, mainly because bacteria think of these things as lunch. Occasionally we do find fossilized remains of soft tissue, but only in places where decay is slow, like hot, dry deserts where bacteria don't live.

Most fossils that are found are of marine animals or plants, since they were most likely to be in or near the water to begin with. But there are also great areas like the Madera County dump or the famous La Brea Tar Pits, where rich deposits of animal fossils have been found.

STICKY GRAVES OF LA BREA

Thousands of fossils have been found in these gooey tar pits located in Los Angeles, California. The natural asphalt tar worked much the same way that mud did underwater; when prehistoric animals wandered into the tar, they got stuck, sank to the bottom of the pit, and died. The tar protected their bodies from bacteria and decay, and within a couple of thousands of years or so—presto change-o—they became fossils!

Elephant Evolution

Ever wonder if elephants—the largest living land animals—always looked the way they do now? Fossils tell the tale. Today's living elephants are survivors of an ancient, more widespread and varied group that evolved from pig-sized ancestors of the Upper Eocene. Here are some of the major stages in elephant evolution:

Moeritherium, who lived between 20 and 40 million years ago, is the oldest of the elephant species. No larger than an everyday hog, this animal had four legs, a tail—and no trunk.

Deinotherium came next. He lived between 1 and 25 million years ago. He looked similar to his ancestor, but had developed a small trunk and slightly larger ears than moeritherium.

Gomphotherium roamed the earth between 10 and 20 million years ago. He was bigger than his ancestors and bore a trunk and tusks, but his ears were still quite small.

Mastodon was next up the evolutionary ladder. He lived 1 million years ago and was similar in most ways to the elephants of today—except for those ears again. They were less than one-fourth of the size we see on modern elephants.

The African elephant is today's most common species and is a good ten times the size of its earliest ancestor!

ENVIRONMENT

Animal remains aren't the only kinds of fossils around, either. Footprints and tracks can also harden into fossils. Did you ever make a handprint or footprint in clay or plaster when you were a little kid? Then you've probably got a pretty good idea of how fossil footprints and other impressions were created. Imprints of bodies, outlines of leaves, and the wingspan of the earliest bird known all left behind fossil impressions in rocks and give us insights into life long ago.

Scientists who study ancient life are called paleontologists, and fossils are their principal clues. Paleontologist Howell Thomas was happy to show our two adventurers around the Madera excavation—and to get a little free labor out of them, too!

Although some paleontologists occasionally find complete skeletons, Vivek discovered that those kinds of "glamour finds" are actually pretty rare. A few scattered bones or the imprint of an ancient leaf are much more common discoveries, and they still give scientists a glimpse of what our earth looked like millions of years ago.

At the Madera landfill excavation, the fossils were from many different animals that had all died in the same place. Looking at their remains was like looking at a snapshot of ancient history. The workers were especially psyched when they discovered that some of the fossils there were from a baby woolly mammoth. Babies in fossil form are rarer than rare since animals grow up pretty quickly in the wild and spend most of their lives as adults. To find a baby anything in the fossil record is an extremely unusual event. And this time *Name Your Adventure* was there!

Many thousands of years ago, the woolly mammoth, with its long, sweeping hair, was a prime subject for cave painters. Complete bodies of the woolly mammoth—just like the one in the University of California at Berkeley Museum of Paleontology that Jordan showed to *Name Your Adventure* viewers—have been found to confirm the accuracy of these drawings.

Woolly mammoths were tall, thin-bodied giants with high heads and tremendous curving tusks. Most stood twelve feet at the shoulders, but one North American species stood a full fourteen feet! The greatest number of mammoth skeletons has been found in the flatlands of the United States, in Montana, North Dakota, South Dakota, and especially in Nebraska.

Mammoths lived during the great Ice Age and had a covering of thick hair in order to keep out the cold. They died out about ten thousand years ago, leaving only the elephants we see today in India and Africa.

ENVIRONMENT

JUST HOW OLD IS THE EARTH?

Besides giving us information about specific animals and plants, fossils are also a testament to the age of the earth. Just how old is the earth? Glad you asked! Look at it this way. If you could compress the whole history of the earth into twenty-four hours, humans would have only been around since about 11:59 P.M. Compared to the history of the entire earth, we've been around less than a minute! That kind of puts us in our place, doesn't it?! But fossils have been around since about 5:20 A.M.—or for about 3,500 million years. The earth itself, of course, is much older than that—probably about 4,500 million years old.

Why don't we have any fossils from that time? Because it was simply too hot on the surface of the earth for anything to survive.

By the time of the Mesozoic era, about 225 million years ago (give or take a day or two), things had cooled down a lot. Seed-bearing trees and flowering plants appeared. And the giant reptiles that we know as dinosaurs were able to roam the earth without the luxury of air-conditioning.

The Mesozoic era gave way to the Cenozoic era—"The Time of Recent Life"—somewhere around 65 million years ago. Most of the animals that had lived before this time had already become extinct, including the mighty dinosaurs. Woolly mammoths like the one discovered in the Madera dig came from this period. The strange new mammals that appeared at the beginning of the Cenozoic era have evolved into the familiar creatures we know today, such as cats, dogs, horses, and elephants. The first humans also appeared. Prehuman fossils have been found that are at least 5 million years old.

Nobody knows for sure why some animals and plants died out completely while others stayed on earth for millions of years. A lot of evolution (the theory that animals and plants develop from earlier forms with slight variations through the years) is a question of good fortune. Often the plants and animals that evolved were simply lucky. By fulfilling a role that few other animals performed, or by living in a place where there wasn't much competition for food, they didn't have as much difficulty surviving as some of their less-lucky neighbors.

Sharks, for instance, have been swimming in the oceans for hundreds of millions of years. They hit on a design which was good and has worked well for them.

Other creatures were simply design failures— lemons that needed to go back to the drawing board. The saber-toothed cat, for example, lived 40 million years ago and had a major problem with its enormous front teeth. These fangs could grow up to seven feet or longer and could end up weighing so much that the cat couldn't even open its mouth!

The history of life is about lots and lots of changes. There have been many extinction events, all related to big environmental changes, in which hundreds of thousands of species have died off. One such cataclysmic event occurred 250 million years ago, at the end of the Permian period. Scientists are still debating about what kind of event it was, but roughly 96 percent of all marine species went extinct.

When there's an environmental change, only the plants and animals that are able to adapt to the new climate can survive. And if the change is drastic, extinction is often the result.

LIVING FOSSILS

There are some animals, though, that don't seem to have needed to change much at all, never died out, and are still with us today. These "living fossils," like the starfish and the horseshoe crab, look almost the same today as they did hundreds of millions of years ago.

Turtles have also changed very little since the prehistoric times. Their hard shells have protected them for 175 million years. The Archelon, the biggest turtle that ever lived, swam in the ocean about 100 million years ago. It grew to be eleven feet long—that's as big as an automobile—and was an ancestor to the turtles of today.

Clams, oysters, and squids also look about the same as they did 400 million years ago. And cockroaches were hanging out with the dinosaurs long before they were scurrying around your kitchen; they're almost 300 million years old! The modern cockroach is about half the size of its prehistoric ancestor, however. Thank goodness! Many of these living fossils help scientists determine what prehistoric creatures may have looked like.

There's a lot of educated guesswork behind our commonly accepted notions of what dinosaurs and mammoths looked like. That's because while small animal fossils are often found completely intact, the remains of larger animals, like dinosaurs, have often been scattered, and often only a few bones are found at any specific dig site.

To form a complete image, paleontologists have to piece together fossils like a jigsaw puzzle. But since they rarely have all the puzzle pieces, they often have to compare their own fossil fragments with existing fossil records, or else look to related animals that are alive today for clues.

That's exactly what happened when paleontologists first discovered the remains of the Parasaurolophus dinosaur. The fossils showed that it had a large hollow

Fabulous Fossil Finds

The biggest intact (whole) fossils ever discovered were of mammoths. They were found in Siberia and Alaska, where the frozen ground completely refrigerated them for years. In Poland, a woolly rhinoceros dating back to the Ice Age was preserved in asphalt. Ground sloths have been preserved in caves.

The smallest fossils found are of insects. From studying them, we have learned that insects account for three-quarters of all living animals!

The rarest fossils found today are those of humans.

The oldest bird fossil ever found was discovered in limestone in Bavaria. The bird, dating from the Jurassic era, was named Archaeopteryx.

The least changed of all creatures includes the horseshoe crab and the cockroach. Both look pretty much the same today as they did millions of years ago.

The most changed of all creatures includes horses and elephants.

One of the most impressive finds of all time took place in Bernissart, Belgium, in 1878, completely by accident. Coal miners, working a thousand feet below ground, unwittingly dug a shaft through the skeleton of a huge animal, almost destroying it before they realized what they'd done. A paleontologist was called to the scene. He identified the bones as the remains of iguanodons (plant-eating dinosaurs)— lots and lots of them! All told, buried beneath the ground were ten complete iguanodon skeletons and many other partial skeletons. Nothing like it had ever been seen before; and a find of this magnitude has never been repeated. It is on display at the Royal Institute in Brussels, Belgium.

structure that stuck up above its head, but scientists couldn't figure out what it was for. Perhaps a bad Mesozoic hair day or a prehistoric ponytail? Comparing the remains of the fossils with animals that are around today, they theorized that the knob might have helped the Parasaurolophus breathe underwater, enhance its sense of smell, or call to other dinosaurs like a trumpeter. Still, the best they could do was make an educated guess.

In fact, Howell helped Vivek do just that after he unearthed his own fossil. When Vivek first pulled his fossil out of the ground he felt a major adrenaline rush because it was the first time he had ever seen or touched a fossil. But just what kind of fossil was it? Howell thought it was probably a horse bone. To find out, they made use of the University of California at Berkeley's Museum of Paleontology fossil collection, the largest collection in the world—like a "library for fossils"—with drawers and drawers filled with fossils. When they went to the collection drawer where the horse bones were and did an actual comparison, ta-da—perfect match!

THE EVOLUTION OF THE HORSE

One of the best-known stories in evolution is the history of the horse. The first horses appeared 55 million years ago, and many hundreds of fossil horses have been collected in the rocks. The first horse was the size of a small dog and was called *Eohippus*, or "dawn horse." It had four toes on each front foot and three toes on each hind—and it sure wasn't much good for riding.

About 37 million years ago, a newcomer called *Mesohippus*, or "middle horse," appeared. These guys were about the size of a German shepherd, and all four feet had three toes. Both the *Eohippus* and the *Mesohippus* lived in the forest and had teeth designed for eating leaves and tender shoots.

It was 25 million years ago when another newcomer, the *Merychippus*, meaning "cud-chewing horse," came into the picture. This guy was about the size of a Great Dane and had powerful jaws and teeth that could grind up food even tougher than leaves. This new and improved model of horse left the forest and grazed on the plains.

From the *Merychippus* came several other types of horses, all of which became extinct except for *Pliohippus*, which means "more of a horse." This horse came around 10 million years ago and was bigger than its ancestors. The *Pliohippus* had one main toe on each foot, as do modern horses. It actually looked similar to the horse of today, *Equus*, which finally evolved about 2 million years ago.

A PURPLE POLKA-DOTTED PARASAUROLOPHUS

Howell opened one of the fossil drawers and showed Vivek and Jordan a frontal piece of a skull from a *Tyrannosaurus rex*. But knowing what the dinosaurs actually looked like is also a whole lot of guesswork. We have no records of the skin or muscles that went over their bones. We don't have their ears, eyes, or noses, nor do we even know for sure where they go.

Paleontologists guess the color of dinosaurs from their modern relatives like the crocodile, but nobody knows for sure if they really were the green, scaly giants that we know from *Jurassic Park*. Some paleontologists think dinosaurs may have had brightly colored skin, perhaps as a form of camouflage. Can you picture a fifty-foot-long, bright yellow Tyrannosaurus with brown polka dots? Maybe that's how they looked. Or what about a Torosaurus, one of the last dinosaurs to appear, with pink-and-purple stripes? It could be true! (Stranger things have happened—just think about some of the outfits that your mother wants you to wear!)

Luckily, not all paleontology is guesswork, and the rock in which fossils are found can provide some concrete clues about when and where the animal may have lived. If you find a fossil in light gray limestone, you know it was deposited in a fairly shallow, warm sea. If you find a dinosaur bone in a red, pebbly bed, you can be pretty

ENVIRONMENT

sure that you're dealing with something that was deposited on land, probably in a stream. And if you ask your friendly neighborhood geologist to measure the rock's radioactivity, you can even figure out how long the rock and the fossil have been around.

But how do paleontologists know where to look for fossils in the first place? After all, the people at Madera County were looking to make another landfill, not a major mammoth find.

Because there were so many different plants and animals around millions of years ago, fossils can be found just about everywhere. What you want to find plays a key role in where you start looking. Dinosaur bones aren't as commonly found as you might think, but most paleontologists know where to look for them because most places where fossils have been found have been recorded. If a paleontologist is interested in finding why the dinosaur became extinct, she may want to go to an area that is really well known for collecting dinosaur fossils—a place where people have been working a lot so there's a lot of detailed knowledge about that area. Then she can begin digging up answers to her specific questions about evolution.

IN SEARCH OF DINOSAURS

Over the course of several summers in the 1980s, the

Our hosts, hunky Mario Lopez and wacky (and not too bad looking) Jordan Brady, grin at the camera.

Rick, Jordan, and oceanographer Steve Miller dive deep into the ocean and collect water samples.

Reef adventurer Rick Sage and Jordan grin through a porthole in the *Aquarius*.

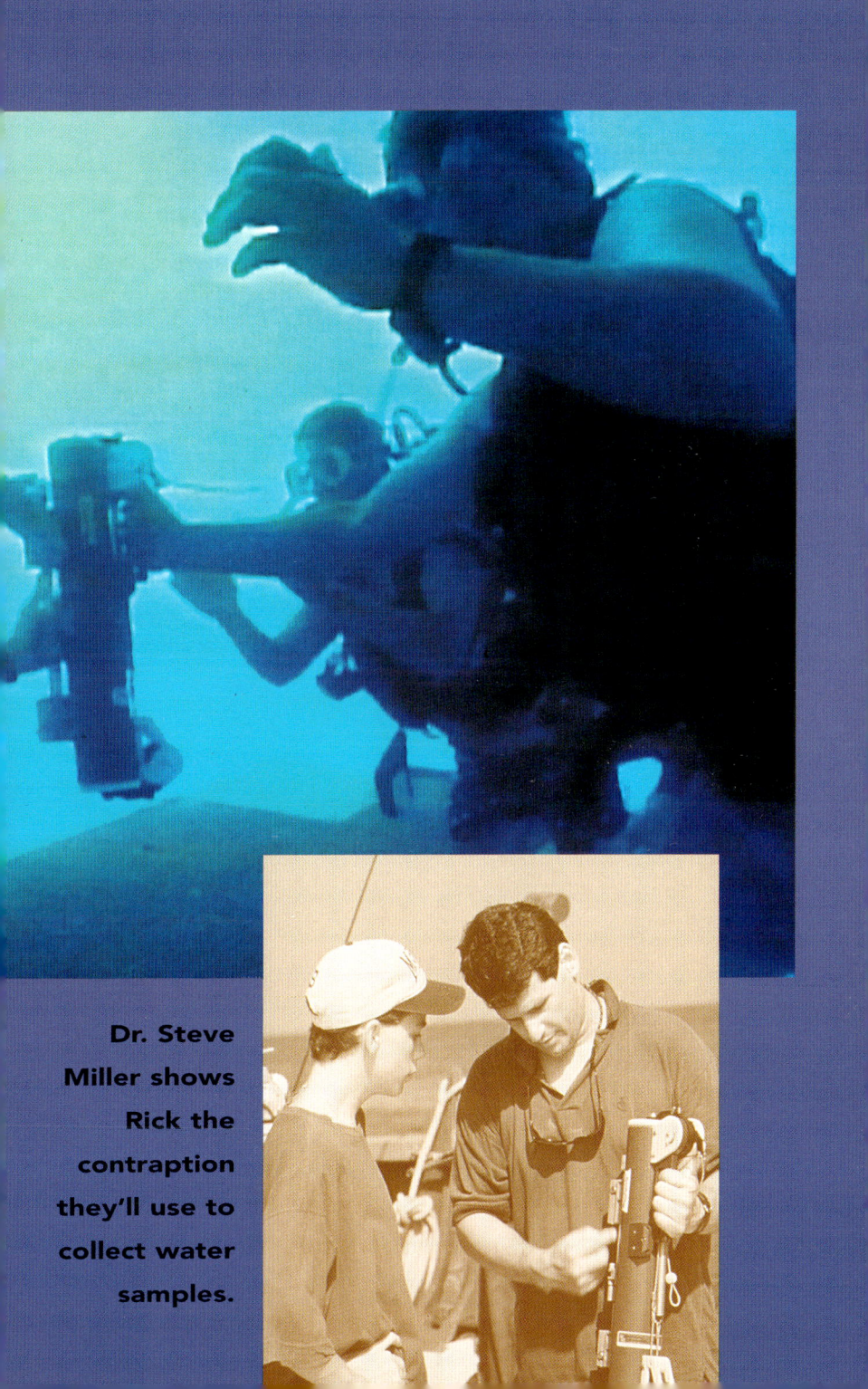

Dr. Steve Miller shows Rick the contraption they'll use to collect water samples.

Rick and Jordan get geared up for their dive with Paige Gill.

Rick and Jordan check out a brain coral in a healthy coral reef—way cool!

Rick and Jordan at the end of their adventure—it's been awesome!

Jordan and paleontology adventurer Vivek Varughese hanging out at the Madera dig site. What's that on your nose, Jordan?

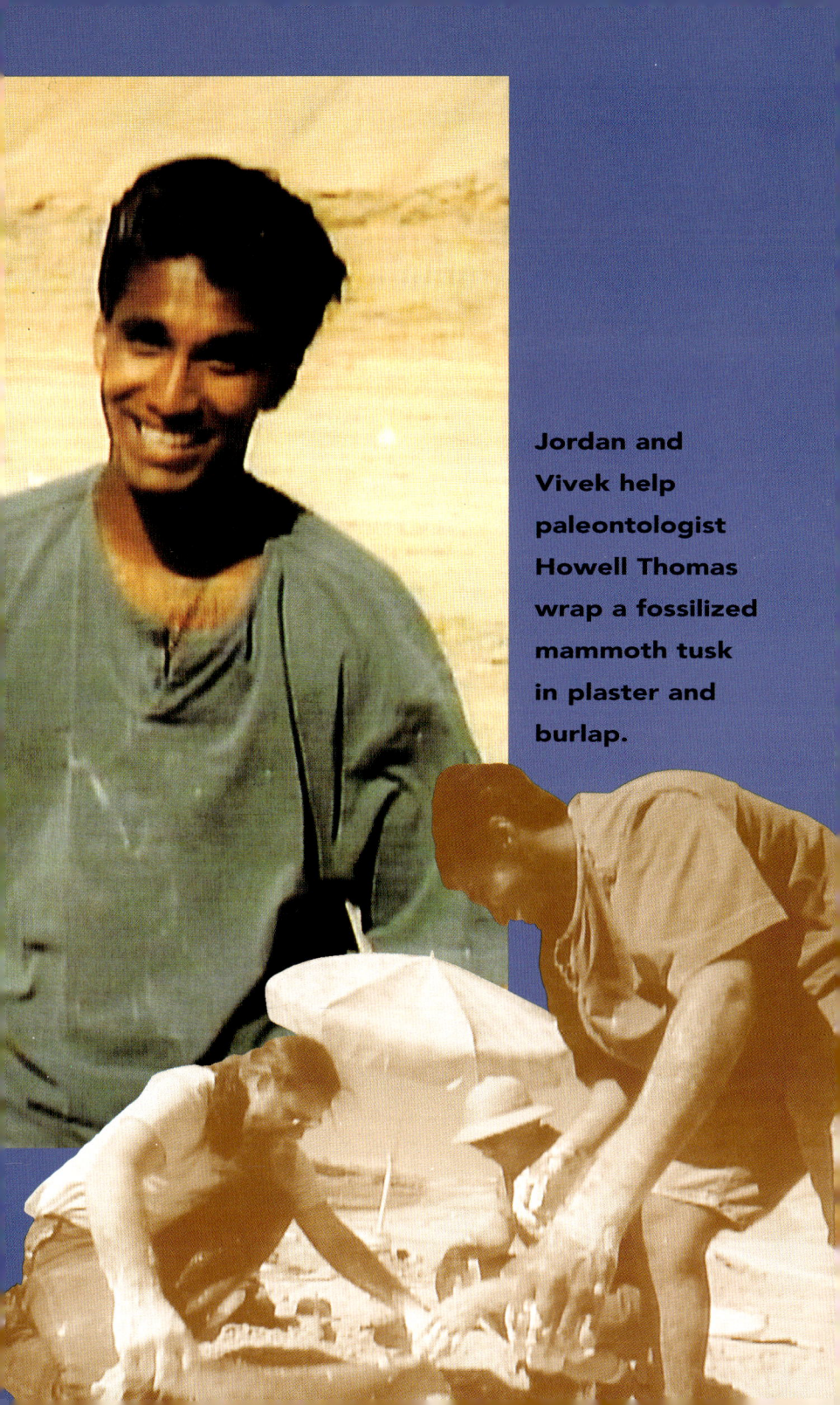

Jordan and Vivek help paleontologist Howell Thomas wrap a fossilized mammoth tusk in plaster and burlap.

Vivek uses a special drill to carefully chip away the dirt around a fossil.

Famous Folks Fascinated with Fossils

If you're interested in fossils and paleontology, you're part of a pretty distinguished group. Several names you'll recognize from history were serious "rock hounds." For instance . . .

Thomas Jefferson wrote about the history of extinct animals before he became president in 1801. While in office a few years later, he reportedly instructed army officers Lewis and Clark not only to map out a land route to the Pacific, but to keep an eye out for living descendants of fossil creatures. But all Lewis and Clark found were more fossils—not the creatures themselves.

Jules Verne, the French novelist, and Ray Bradbury, the famous science fiction writer, are just two of many authors whose amateur study of fossils has influenced their work. Verne's "Journey to the Center of the Earth" was fiction, but in spinning his fabulous tale of subterranean exploration, he used his extensive knowledge of geology and paleontology to make it all seem very real! And Bradbury creates fantastic, fearsome creatures from the depths of prehistory in his sci-fi tales, drawing on his expertise of fossils.

Leonardo da Vinci, the multi-faceted Renaissance era artist, was intrigued by fossils. He observed sedimentary rock layers and was the first person of his time to refute the strictly religious explanation of such phenomena and take a scientific stand on the issue.

Andrew Carnegie is known for being a wealthy industrialist and philanthropist. But the people of France also know him as the man who, in 1908, gave them a very special gift—a cast of the first Diplodocus ever to be reconstructed. (Mr. Carnegie financed the expedition on which these fossils were found.) The dinosaur skeleton stands over eighty-eight feet tall and is on permanent display at the National Museum of History in Paris.

ENVIRONMENT

Milwaukee Public Museum organized a dig in North and South Dakota. Paleontologists and civilians searched for dinosaur bones in order to try and figure out how the dinosaurs became extinct. They looked through a series of rocks across an area where they knew several species of dinosaurs lived and died, and tried to answer two questions: How many bones were from dinosaurs that died while other dinosaurs still lived? And how many were from the dinosaur extinction?

Another question they were looking to answer: Was the decline of the dinosaur gradual, or does it appear to have been very abrupt?

To do that kind of work you need lots of people wandering over large areas of land counting up how many bones they find. It was, without doubt, an enormous project, probably one of the biggest in terms of intensity and number of people doing paleontology.

It's not unusual to have a couple of dozen people all involved in the same fossil dig, as at the Madera County dig. There were scientists from all three branches of paleontology uncovering bits of the past in the hot California sun. There were the vertebrate paleontologists—Howell's area of expertise—who study bones. Then there were the invertebrate paleontologists—those are the guys who study animals that don't have bones.

And then there were the paleobotanists, who study plants.

But paleontologists can also work alone. If the paleontologist is not familiar with the area he plans on exploring, he can always hire a local amateur. It's not hard to find amateurs like Vivek who are willing to lend a hand. And as *Name Your Adventure* discovered, you don't have to know everything about paleontology just to work at a dig (that explains how Jordan got there!). Most of the work at an excavation is just that: work—hard, sweaty, dirty work.

You don't even have to hook up with a paleontologist to go fossil hunting. You can find your own dig site by checking a geological survey map for areas that were once underwater. Stop by your local library and do some research to find out what fossils have been found in your area and where.

Since most fossils were formed underwater, the best place to start looking is in areas that were once submerged. Riverbanks and cliffs are perfect. Or if a new road has been dug through a nearby hill, half your work has already been done for you. But remember, it's a good idea to bring an adult along with you. You'll need someone to drive you from place to place, and to hold all the fossils you find!

When you go out in search of fossils, be sure to

Fun with Fossils

What's so cool about being a rock hound? Glad you asked!

1. It's a pretty original hobby—there are many more stamp collectors than there are fossil hunters!
2. You can do it year-round (unless the ground is covered with snow).
3. It takes you out of doors and off the beaten track.
4. You learn about the land where you live really well.
5. You get to hang out with other rock hounds.
6. It's a puzzle lover's delight—there are so many unsolved fossil mysteries to tackle.
7. Fossils reconstruct life—they enable scientists to accurately picture many kinds of long-extinct plants and animals.
8. Fossils plot geography—they indicate ancient land and water areas and show the changing continents.
9. Fossils that are indexed establish the time relationship between rocks of different areas.
10. Fossils are natural resources: They're a source of coal, oil, lime, phosphate, and building stones.
11. You might stumble onto a major discovery!

dress properly. Rough outdoor clothing and waterproof boots are always a good start. Vivek and Jordan soon discovered that paleontology can be a hot, sweaty, dusty business, so leave your Armani suit at home! Always wear protective glasses or goggles when you're chipping away at the rocks. And be sure to bring plenty of sunscreen.

You'll need to bring along some special tools on your fossil-finding expedition, too, unless you plan to rely on your superhuman strength to rip apart the rocks. Paleontologists use hammers with a flat edge that you can find at any hobby or hardware store. You'll also need some chisels in your tool belt, but make sure they're cold steel chisels, not the type used to work with wood. If there's an ice pick around the house, that's also a useful tool. At the Madera County dig, that's what Vivek used to dig a trench around the baby mammoth's tusk so it could easily be removed from the soil.

Okay, Indiana Jones, now you're ready to dig, but hold on to your pith helmet for half a second first. You're not going to have much luck if you go up to any old rock and whack it with your hammer. Choose your location carefully, and then go about it systematically. If you dig down gradually, making your way through the layers of earth in an orderly fashion, you'll see a lot more rock and find a lot more fossils. Fossils aren't hard to spot. They're usually a different color from the rock around them. Some may stick out from the rock or you may even recognize a feature, such as a shell.

Once you find your fossil, then it's time to remove it from the rock with your hammer and chisel. But be careful not to break the rock or the fossil. Chip away at the rock, about an inch or two from where the fossil is.

Once you've got it out, the first thing to do is wrap it with some toilet paper that you brought from home. This is called jacketing. A fossil is jacketed to make sure it doesn't break while being transported back to the lab or your home. A couple of layers of TP, a little bit of water, and a casing of burlap made Vivek's fossil look like some sort of enormous prehistoric spitball!

Remember to label any fossils that you find right away, just like the scientists do. Sure, you may think you've got this great memory and that labeling's a waste of time—until a few hours pass, then you hike home, throw down your backpack, grab a snack, and watch a little TV. By the time you get around to unpacking your fossil find, you suddenly realize that you can't remember exactly where you found it! Don't be a bonehead about your bones; always label them with the place where they were found and the date.

When you get back home, remove the rest of the

rock and dirt from your fossil. Make sure your work space has lots of light, and that your parents won't go ballistic about the mess. Gently brush off bits of rock and dust with a paintbrush, and try using a dental pick or small screwdriver to get into every nook and cranny.

You can even wash your fossil if you're very careful. Use a mild soap and blow it dry with a hair dryer (no mousse, please!), or gently buff it with a soft cloth to give it a good shine for when you want to show it off.

Mark Goodman, a scientist at the University of California at Berkeley's Museum of Paleontology, showed Vivek and Jordan how he removed rock and dirt from a sloth skull found at the Madera dig. In the lab he used a small needle and carefully scraped all the dirt and sand away from the bone. Once the bone was exposed, he brushed glue on the skull. The bone absorbed the glue and hardened from the inside out to preserve it better. Vivek got to put this knowledge to work when Mark gave him his own jacketed fossil to work on.

KEEPING TRACK OF ALL THOSE FOSSILS

Scientists at the University of California at Berkeley's Museum of Paleontology log their fossil finds into their computer systems. They include information about the

ENVIRONMENT

number of fossils found, how they were acquired, when, and by whom. They also list where each fossil was found and in what type of rock.

You can do the same thing in your own room. Keep a list of all the different fossils that you've found. Mention the area you found them in. Did you find the fossil in a sandy area or in dirt? How many fossils did you find that day? Would it be a good idea to go back to the same area? Any information that would help you out should be recorded.

If you're not quite sure what type of fossil you have found—and you don't have a museum fossil library at your disposal as Vivek did—there are lots of different publications at the library you can turn to for help.

It's very rare these days to find a type of fossil that is totally new. Almost everything has been identified. If you can't find your particular fossil in a textbook, go to a museum and ask if you can look in their fossil drawers. Look for another fossil that closely resembles yours. If you have any questions, you can ask one of the paleontologists on staff for more help.

There's little chance that Vivek will ever forget his exciting day as a paleontologist or what he learned during his adventure. He had never been to an actual site where dinosaurs or mammoths or any ancient creatures died. He had never participated in a dig or been inside a lab where fossils were taken out. And he'd never seen a real skeleton of a dinosaur before, all of which he got to do simply by writing to *Name Your Adventure.*

"I'm definitely more excited about being a paleontologist now because I know more about what the scientists actually do and how interesting it really is," Vivek told the *Name Your Adventure* viewers. "It's a really great field to go into."

No doubt Vivek will become a paleontologist and get to put his fossil finds on display for people to see and learn from. He already has one fossil to his credit. Howell put Vivek's fossil in the display case at the University of California at Berkeley's Museum of Paleontology, right above a plaque with his name on it!

So *Name Your Adventure* played a major part in discovering a fossil and you were right there—only you didn't have to get dirty! If you'd like to learn more about paleontology, fossils, or Vivek's good-looking hair (okay, maybe not his hair), go to a museum.

Recycling—Putting Natural Resources to Work

What kind of lame weirdo would want to spend an afternoon at a dump?

That's what Jordan first wondered when he heard that he was going to meet Bahar Soomekh, a seventeen-year-old environmental crusader. He soon discovered, though, that the "dump" was actually a plastic recycling center and that Bahar was not some crazed enviro-weenie. In fact, her goal is to be an environmental reporter, and the refresher course that she gave to Jordan on the three R's just shows how golden her future is going to be!

Jordan was already hip to the environmental three R's—Reduce, Reuse, and Recycle—but Bahar still taught him a lot. For instance, the average American throws out three to four pounds of trash a day. Did you know that you'll probably create about six hundred times your adult weight in trash during your lifetime? That's a meg-amountain of rotting rubbish! Almost 40 percent of that will be in the form of packaging—envelopes and cartons that you probably didn't even need in the first place!

How can you reduce all that waste? The simplest way is to keep an eye on the amount of packaging a product has. If you have to open a box, take out a package, and unwrap that package just to get at the product you've bought, you've just wasted a lot of natural resources, a lot of energy, and a lot of time. If you don't need all that packaging, send a message to the manufacturer by not buying that product.

Instead of throwing things away after only one use, reuse them. Reuse is number two. Use cups made of glass or plastic that can be washed and reused instead of drinking from paper. Take your grocery bags back to the store. They'll carry just as much the second time around. Rinse out the small bags you use to hold fruits and veggies and use them again, too.

And finally, the third R: Recycle. Recycling lets us make new things out of the old. The more we recycle, the less we rob the earth of its limited natural resources. And Bahar was the right person to talk to about recycling. In fact, she's practically a recycling genius!

Bahar started out small by recycling paper, aluminum cans, and newsprint at her high school. But then things started to snowball, and soon she and her friends were organizing an environmental fair for ten other schools! Their focus? Recycling, of course—which is how Jordan came to be floundering in a mountain of recy-

ENVIRONMENT

clable milk jugs at a Los Angeles recycling plant, where recycling expert Caroline Renee walked Jordan and Bahar through the process that transforms yesterday's milk jugs into tomorrow's soda bottle.

First, the plastics must be sorted out according to type. This is one job where you want to be sure to wear your rubber gloves and bring a clothespin for your nose! Even though recyclable plastic is supposed to be rinsed out before collection, not everybody remembers to do it, and the odors can get pretty rank!

There are seven different types of plastic that can be recycled. To help simplify the sorting process, every plastic bottle or container must have a number on the bottom that tells what type of plastic it is.

PLASTICS PLUS

So you think you're pretty hip to recycling plastic? Well, let's journey into the exciting game-show world of "Name Your Plastics" and see just how much you really know.

If you had a bottle with a number one and "PETE" written on the bottom or side of the container, would you (a) have a bottle that used to belong to Pete or (b) would the letters stand for Polyethylene Terethalate? If you answered b, you're absolutely correct! This type of plastic is used for soda bottles, like those two-liter plas-

Shop Talk—How to Do Your Recycling Bit at the Mall

BYOB: Bring your own bag—one bag, that is. Think about it: At each store you hit, they give you a bag for your purchase. Pretty soon, you've got a serious bunch of bags that you're just going to throw away. The solution is simple. Bring your own cool canvas carryall and tell the cashier: "No thanks, I don't need a bag, just the receipt." Just remember to get a bag or backpack that's big enough for everything you're buying.

At the card shop, buy greeting cards that are printed on recycled paper.

Ignore the temptation to buy one-time-use disposables, like plastic razors.

Remember Mom and Dad—give them nice, big, reusable coffee mugs to take to work. That way they won't have to use Styrofoam.

Think big when it comes to nonperishables—buying the bigger size cuts down on packaging. So make it one big cereal box instead of several small ones; one huge peanut butter tub; and can the six-pack in favor of a big, two-liter bottle of soda.

tic bottles. It's also used for see-through containers such as mouthwash and hand soap dispensers. This plastic is generally clear or green.

Okay, time for survey question number two. If there's a number two on the bottom of a bottle, which is what most shampoo bottles have, is the bottle made from plastic known as (a) high-density polyethylene or (b) HDPE? Well, that was a trick question. The correct answer is a and b. This plastic can be colorful (white, yellow, pink, orange) or have no color, like the clear milk jugs.

To see what these numbers look like and how they're used, check out the bottles in your house. You'll see a chasing arrow—the recycling symbol. Inside the recycling symbol there will be a number that identifies the plastic.

Once the plastic is sorted by number, it's conveyor-belt time. From here it enters a large machine that's like an electric baby brother: It chews up whatever you put in it, then spits it out in a million tiny pieces. A cold wash removes any paper or labels that may still be clinging to the shredded plastic, and a hot wash with detergent cleans and disinfects the pieces. (By the way, even the "dishwater" gets recycled here. A sewage treatment plant removes the chemicals and soap before discharging the water back into its natural water source.)

The plastic pieces are then shaken to remove some

of the water before they go to the dryers (sort of like what your golden retriever does after its bath!). At last, the clean plastic chips are melted down and molten plastic goo is shaped into long, thin tubes that look like spaghetti. But hold the marinara sauce! These plastic strands are then chopped up into same-size pellets. These pellets can then be sold, melted down again into a plastic glop that resembles chewing gum, and formed into something useful, like a detergent bottle or a grocery bag. Shred it, scrub it, melt it, and mold it, and suddenly something old is something new again!

The plastic companies are now making things even easier by developing products that can be made from recycled plastic. In the United States, we throw away 2.5 million plastic bottles every hour. That's right, every hour! Right now, only about 2 percent of all the plastics that

> **Make that Six R's**
>
> You've already read about the three R's: Reduce, Reuse, Recycle. We'd like to add three more:
> Rinse those containers you're about to toss into the recycling bin.
> Remove metal caps from jars.
> Respond enthusiastically and immediately to the recycling efforts in your town and school and at home.

ENVIRONMENT

Glass Recycling Made Easy

Most people know that glass is recyclable. But most people don't realize that not all glass is created equal when it comes to recycling. So clip this list and paste it up in your kitchen.

<u>Recycle Me, Please</u>
Soda bottles, beer bottles, juice containers, ketchup bottles, wine and liquor bottles, food containers

<u>Sorry, I Can't Be Recycled</u>
Ceramic beer and wine caps, ceramic cups and plates, clay flowerpots, crystal, lightbulbs, mirror and window glass, heat-resistant ovenware, drinking glasses

are being made are being recycled. Plastic manufacturers are using recycled plastic to make a number of interesting products, such as plastic lumber and fiberfill for sleeping bag insulation.

Okay, that's recycling plastic, but what about the 28 billion glass bottles and jars we throw away each year? That's enough glass to fill the twin towers of New York's World Trade Center! Luckily, glass can also be recycled—a good thing, since it takes practically forever to decompose. The ketchup bottle you threw away last week could still be littering up a landfill in the year 3000!

Unlike plastic, glass is sorted by color, not code, and collection centers will only accept glass that has already been sorted. Sure, it would be easier if we could just throw all our bottles into one big pile, but it just doesn't work that way. The color of the recycled glass would end up being a dark, smoky gray—not very attractive or appetizing for jelly jars, ketchup bottles, and other food containers.

People have been making glass for nearly 3,500 years, using three basic ingredients: white sand, soda, and lime. All three are plentiful (just check your sneakers after a walk on the beach!), and pretty cheap, too. So what's the big deal about recycling? It's because all three must be mined and transported, using way too much energy.

To make glass, sand, soda, and lime are heated together until they completely dissolve and become transparent. Then the mixture is cooled and hardened into glass. Before it's shipped off to manufacturers, it's broken into "cullet"—small pieces of glass, whether new or recycled.

Recycled glass is run through a machine to remove any plastic rings from old bottles. A vacuum process sucks off plastic coatings and paper labels and the glass is broken into small pieces. Now the cullet is ready to be heated or added to new cullet to be made into bottles, glasses, or jars. Recycled glass is even being used to make road paint and a new paving material called "glassphalt." By mixing glass chips with tar, they're actu-

ENVIRONMENT

ally making roads out of broken bottles—without causing flat tires!

All the bottles and jars that you turn in for recycling are actually used to make new glass. But other kinds of glass, like windowpanes, Pyrex, and lightbulbs, are made by different processes and can't be recycled at glass centers. So if you break a mirror, you probably won't have seven years bad luck, but you will be out of luck as far as recycling it goes.

The Coke can you drained at lunch today is much easier to recycle than anything made out of glass. That's because all aluminum melts at a fairly low heating temperature, making aluminum the most recycled material in the world.

According to the Aluminum Association, Americans recycled 42.5 billion aluminum cans in 1988.

Aluminum is also the most abundant metal on earth and is made from bauxite ore. But it takes six or seven times more energy to create raw aluminum from bauxite ore than it does to recycle used aluminum. Ouch! Talk about an energy crunch. The energy saved from recycling just one aluminum can could run your TV set for three hours. That's three free hours of *Name Your Adventure* just for walking your Coke can over to the recycling bin!

A lot more than cans can be recycled, too, including aluminum foil, pie plates, and frozen food trays. And a recycled aluminum product is generally back in the store within six weeks. So if your Sprite tastes a bit familiar, it may be because part of the can is one you drank from a few months ago.

Aluminum manufacturing companies make $2 million from recycling every day, which is probably why there are more ways to recycle aluminum than any other material. One of the funkiest is reverse vending machines that take your aluminum cans, weigh or count them, then dispense money or tokens in payment. Getting paid to do good—very cool! No wonder this recycling thing is catching on!

Of course, glass, plastic, and aluminum are just a fraction of our recycling responsibilities. Paper is the largest single waste product in America, and it can be recycled, too.

Most paper is made from trees—lots of trees! It takes an entire forest of five hundred thousand trees to supply Americans with their Sunday newspapers every week. In fact, Americans use 50 million tons of paper a year, using up over 850 million trees. Timber-r-r!

Unless we want to end up with an endless prairie—and no more forests—we've got to reduce our paper use. Try tracking your own paper use and see how much paper you throw away that you could have saved or used

Make a Compost Heap!

A compost pile turns leftover foods and other biodegradable garbage into rich soil. Here's how you can make your own.

1. Get an old trash can and put it in an unused, shady part of your yard. (If you don't have a trash can, any container that's at least three feet high, wide, and deep will work as your compost bin.) Ask your parents to drill two rows of holes in the sides, three inches up from the bottom for the first row, then another three inches higher for the second row.

2. Gather small bits of sand, broken pottery, strips of wood, some peat moss from your garden center, and a bunch of earthworms from your garden soil.

3. Layer these things in the can. Place the sand and broken pottery on the bottom, and add the strips of wood. Then toss the peat moss on top. Hang on to those earthworms!

4. Next, add chopped-up waste from fruit and vegetable peels, and put the worms in with the waste food. They'll eat it up and turn it into rich, fertile soil.

5. When you have about six inches of food waste in the can, sprinkle a bit of manure, high-nitrogen fertilizer, or compost activator on top. Continue layering food waste and manure (or fertilizer or compost activator).

6. Once in a while, add enough water to moisten the heap.

7. Cover your compost pile with the garbage can lid or a board. In three to six months you'll have a wonderfully rich soil!

WHAT TO COMPOST

Garden waste, such as weeds, grass clippings, leaves, and plant trimmings

Kitchen waste, such as coffee grinds, crushed eggshells, vegetable and fruit peelings

Shredded newspapers

WHAT NOT TO COMPOST

Animal bones or meat, pits from fruit, fatty foods, dairy products

Grass clippings you've used weed killer or insecticides on; vegetation affected by disease or pests

Metal, plastic, or glass

RECYCLING

again. Could you have tried to write on both sides of the page? Or maybe passed one less note to your friends during study hall? Or how about swapping your *Name Your Adventure* paperbacks at the used bookstore instead of tossing them in the trash?

PAPER TOWEL TIDBIT

Paper towels and toilet paper are often made from recycled paper. About 40 percent of all paper is recycled without any loss of quality.

Paper manufacturers are trying to develop better ways to recycle or reclaim the pulp—the wood material—in paper, but one of their biggest problems is de-inking. Before used pulp can be made into new paper, all the old ink and dyes have to be removed. That can be pretty expensive—so expensive that recycled paper often costs more than paper made directly from trees. And who wants to buy a more expensive product when you can buy perfectly good, unrecycled paper for less?

Realizing this, President Clinton is trying to jump-start the paper-recycling industry by making sure that the federal government sets a good example. The Clinton administration has mandated that all paper purchased by the federal government have at least a 20 percent recycled content by the year 1996. By 1998, that figure jumps up to 30 percent. Considering that federal paper pushers push almost $3 billion worth of paper each year, this new initiative provides a big incentive for paper manufacturers to produce more recycled paper.

So what if you don't throw away three million bucks' worth of paper a year? Can you still make a difference in the big recycling picture? Sure! As Bahar reminded Jordan, "Think globally, act locally," because every little bit can help.

Step one is starting your own recycling center right at home. Set up your garbage so you can conveniently separate and save your recyclables by keeping separate boxes for glass, plastic, and aluminum.

Remove any collars, corks, or metal caps from bottles, but don't worry too much about paper labels—they'll be removed at the recycling plant.

Rinsing is suggested, though isn't absolutely necessary. But do remove any food scraps before you recycle or else your bins will get moldy and gross. As for newspapers, simply stack them beside the rest of your recyclables.

Once you've got a place to put your recyclables, remember to use it. It only takes about fifteen minutes a week to keep up the habit, but forgetting to recycle can affect our earth for centuries to come.

Once a week, properly dispose of your recyclables. Call your local government to find out if curbside recycling is available in your community. If it is, just haul your recyclables to the curb and forget about them! If your town doesn't make recycling pickups, you may be able to drop off your recyclables at supermarkets or shopping centers. Mom or Dad would love the company while they're shopping, and you may even get a special something for being so responsible.

Another option is to take your recyclables to a commercial recycling center. In fact, the batteries you use in your toys, Walkman, and camera should always be taken to a recycling center—*Never throw them away!* Most batteries contain mercury or cadmium—highly toxic sub-

ENVIRONMENT

stances that are major hazardous wastes. When batteries are burned or placed in landfills, these substances are released into the ground or air. Recycling centers may even pay you for your old batteries. Why not take the money and buy rechargeable batteries? Now that's using your head!

Bahar and Jordan are fans of recycling because it makes good economic sense. By reusing our resources, we save energy, money, and the beauty of our planet.

Recycling's also great for your sense of self-esteem. Doing something good for the earth can be a real natural high! But the most compelling reason for recycling is that we're running out of places to stash our trash.

Across the country, almost 90 percent of our garbage is simply dumped and buried in landfills. And at the rate we're generating garbage, we'll soon need five hundred new dumps every year. There's just not enough room! In fact, more than half the cities in America have already exhausted their own landfills.

Couldn't we just burn our trash instead? Sure, but we'd still need to dispose of the ash. Many times, ash is considered hazardous waste because the toxins in our garbage get concentrated when it burns. Other times, toxins get released into the air during incineration. Styrofoam, for example, releases chlorofluorocarbons, or CFCs, into the air when it burns. What's the big deal about CFCs, you ask? Nothing, really, unless you happen to be fond of our ozone layer!

So, we've got way too much trash, dangerous ash, and an ozone layer that's gashed. Suddenly, recycling's looking like a pretty good option. But don't go thinking it's a new idea. Although we've heard a lot about recycling over the past ten years, it's been going on for a very long time. Ask your grandparents (and your great-grandparents) about recycling rubber and metal during the depression and the two world wars. They'll tell you that recycling's not some newfangled fad!

People have always taken scrapped steel and melted it down to make new things. Your very own mountain bike could well have been part of somebody's totaled Porsche at one time!

The milkmen who used to deliver milk door-to-door were also early recyclers. They picked up the empty bottles and took them back to the dairy to be washed and refilled with milk. Ta-da! Recycling in action! Okay, actually they reused the bottles, which is even better than recycling because they didn't have to use more fuel to reform the old glass into new.

300 MILLION TONS OF TRASH!

So how much trash do we actually recycle compared to what we throw away? Glad you asked! Americans

ENVIRONMENT

throw away over 300 million tons of trash a year. That's a rough estimate from Environmental Protection Agency (EPA) statistics. The amount of trash that is recycled varies from place to place. If you live in the Pacific Northwest, where recycling has been going pretty strong for over fifteen years, as much as 25 percent of waste is recycled. In other areas, the only things that get recycled are aluminum cans, and maybe some steel. It really varies depending on where you live and what type of recycling programs are available. Check out your area and see how your city rates.

74 "RECYCLED" VS. "RECYCLABLE"

Just because a product says "recyclable" on the label doesn't mean that it has actually been recycled. "Recyclable" and "recycled" are two different terms. "Recycled" means that the item was once part of the waste stream and has been reused and reformed into a new object.

"Recyclable" means that an object is able to be recycled. But if you don't do your part to recycle it, it doesn't do much good to have the word on the label. Buying a recyclable shampoo bottle is a pretty meaningless gesture if you just throw it away when it's empty and it ends up in a landfill.

Recycling

Now that you're an expert on reducing, reusing, and recycling, share your knowledge with others.

School's a good place to start. That's what Bahar did when she organized her environmental fair—and she raised everyone's awareness. Keep track of how much packaging is used in the cafeteria. Are they selling wrapped hamburgers or plastic bottles of soda and juice that are just being thrown away? Are cups made of biodegradable paper or almost-everlasting Styrofoam?

Take the results to your teachers or principal and share your knowledge with them. Give them real suggestions about how they can make things better.

You could also start a recycling program in your school. Recycling paper is a logical way to begin since schools and offices throw enough of it away to build a twelve-foot wall from Los Angeles to New York every year.

Every classroom can save paper. The trick is to sort it into recyclable groups as it's discarded. Then the custodian can collect it and deposit it in large outdoor containers.

But don't just stop there! Ask your principal or teacher if you can recycle aluminum cans, glass, or other items that your local recycling center accepts. Put the recycling bins in a prominent place in the lunchroom or

ENVIRONMENT

next to the soda machines so that recycling will soon become second nature. And set up a special environmental bulletin board to keep friends in the know about recycling and protecting our planet.

With all we've learned about recycling, remember that it's also important to buy recycled goods. This encourages manufacturers to make and even sell recycled products. Ideally, the label should say "Made with 40 Percent Postconsumer Waste" or "Made with Recycled Material." Of course, not all recycled products have labels—remember Jordan's way-funky briefcase made out of an old Goodyear tire that he carried on the show?

Packaging should be recycled and recyclable as well. For example, most cereal boxes are made of recycled cardboard. It's easy to tell because they're gray inside. But since you can't rip each box open in the store, be sure to look for the recycled logo—the chasing arrows symbol that lets you know that a product is a good environmental choice.

The city of Berkeley, California, actively encourages its residents to buy food packaged in biodegradable or recyclable materials. They call it "precycling," and it may well be the easiest choice you can make to save the earth. Precycling is just as easy as recycling if you keep your eyes open when you shop. It's as simple as asking your family to buy eggs in cardboard, not Styrofoam cartons. Everything you buy has an effect on the environment. Try to make it a positive one.

Having the chance to educate *Name Your Adventure* viewers was a dream come true for Bahar. In true environmental reporter form, she wants everyone to be as aware of the three R's as she is. To make sure that Jordan stayed on the right track, Bahar gave him a pair of 100 percent recycled plastic boots. Bahar knows that it's important to buy recycled goods. Her gift to Jordan encourages manufacturers to sell recycled materials and "close the loop."

As Bahar's adventure drew to a close, she took the time to remind us to think globally, act locally. You might not see firsthand how you're saving the world, but your actions do make a difference—and they will make you feel better and help you stay focused on conservation, just like Bahar.

Rain Forests—
Life under the Canopy

The growls of ferocious beasts echoed beneath the forest canopy . . . something slippery slithered underfoot . . . and the steady drip-drip-drip after a morning cloudburst sounded eerily like drums beating in the distance: *Name Your Adventure* was exploring the vanishing rain forest.

Okay, it wasn't exactly the Amazon, and the only thing growling was Jordan's stomach! But it was wild, it was majestic, and it was Elise Kovar's very own adventure in the temperate rain forest of Oregon.

Oregon? Yes, Oregon! In fact, there are temperate rain forests all up and down the coastal regions of Washington, Oregon, and northern California. If you want to visit a tropical rain forest but still stay on American soil, you'll have to go a little farther afield, to Hawaii, Puerto Rico, the U.S. Virgin Islands, or American Samoa.

Elise flew to Oregon from Los Angeles to check out one of the last American temperate rain forests. She became interested in environmental issues like the rain forest and animal rights (she's even a vegetarian!) when she attended Earth Day. The seventeen-year-old environmentalist wants to help save the planet and figured that the Pacific Northwest was a great place to start.

At one time, rain forests covered over 4 billion acres of the earth (that's nearly twice the size of the United States). Temperate rain forests accounted for 25 million acres. Now, according to Paul Englemeir, a member of the Oregon Natural Resources Council and the Audubon Society (which, Elise and Jordan pointed out, is not just for birds), they're down to only 2.5 million acres. Together, tropical and temperate rain forests cover about 7 percent of the earth. Acid rain, forestry, and farming have all taken their toll on these magnificent ecosystems.

ANYONE GOT AN UMBRELLA?

What makes a rain forest a rain forest? It doesn't take a genius to figure out that one of the major factors is rain. A temperate rain forest actually gets anywhere from 60 to 160 inches of rain a year (a tropical rain forest can get from 80 to 200 inches). In comparison, Chicago gets about 33 inches, and San Francisco receives only 20.

Mild, temperate temperatures aid long growing seasons in temperate rain forests like the one *Name Your Adventure* flew Elise to in Oregon. The ample rain and

ENVIRONMENT

mild climate allow trees to live much longer than trees in other forests. These forests are often referred to as "old growth forests" because many of the trees are very old. Some old forest trees are a thousand years old! Most of the trees are conifers, or cone-bearing trees like pines, spruces, hemlocks, and the Douglas fir, which is the dominant tree in temperate rain forests. These trees are "evergreens," which means they don't shed their leaves.

While conifers may be the dominant type of tree found in these forests, they are not the only trees to grow there. Red alders, which are deciduous trees (ones that shed their leaves in the autumn and grow new leaves in the spring), live a short seventy years. But they can do what few other trees can do—their roots can harbor bacteria that capture nitrogen and store it. When the alders die, they release this nitrogen into the air, which helps the growing conifers reach their tremendous heights.

Many people confuse rain forests with jungles, but they are two completely different things. For one thing, you don't run across many jungles in the Pacific Northwest! Seriously, though, jungles have extremely dense undergrowth that makes walking next to impossible, but rain forests are much more open and easier to move about in. Jordan and Elise didn't have to thrash

Jordan greets Bahar Soomekh, an environmental crusader and recycler extraordinaire!

A recycling expert gives Jordan and Bahar a quick lesson in plastics.

Jordan and Elise Kovar carefully handle a western red cedar, affectionately called Bertha (Thank you, Jordan!).

Elise measures a towering tree in the rain forest. It's so big the measuring tape won't go all the way around!

Jordan and Elise take a hike in the rain forest—check out that view!

Renee Gragnano holds a dolphin in the water—and they're both smiling!

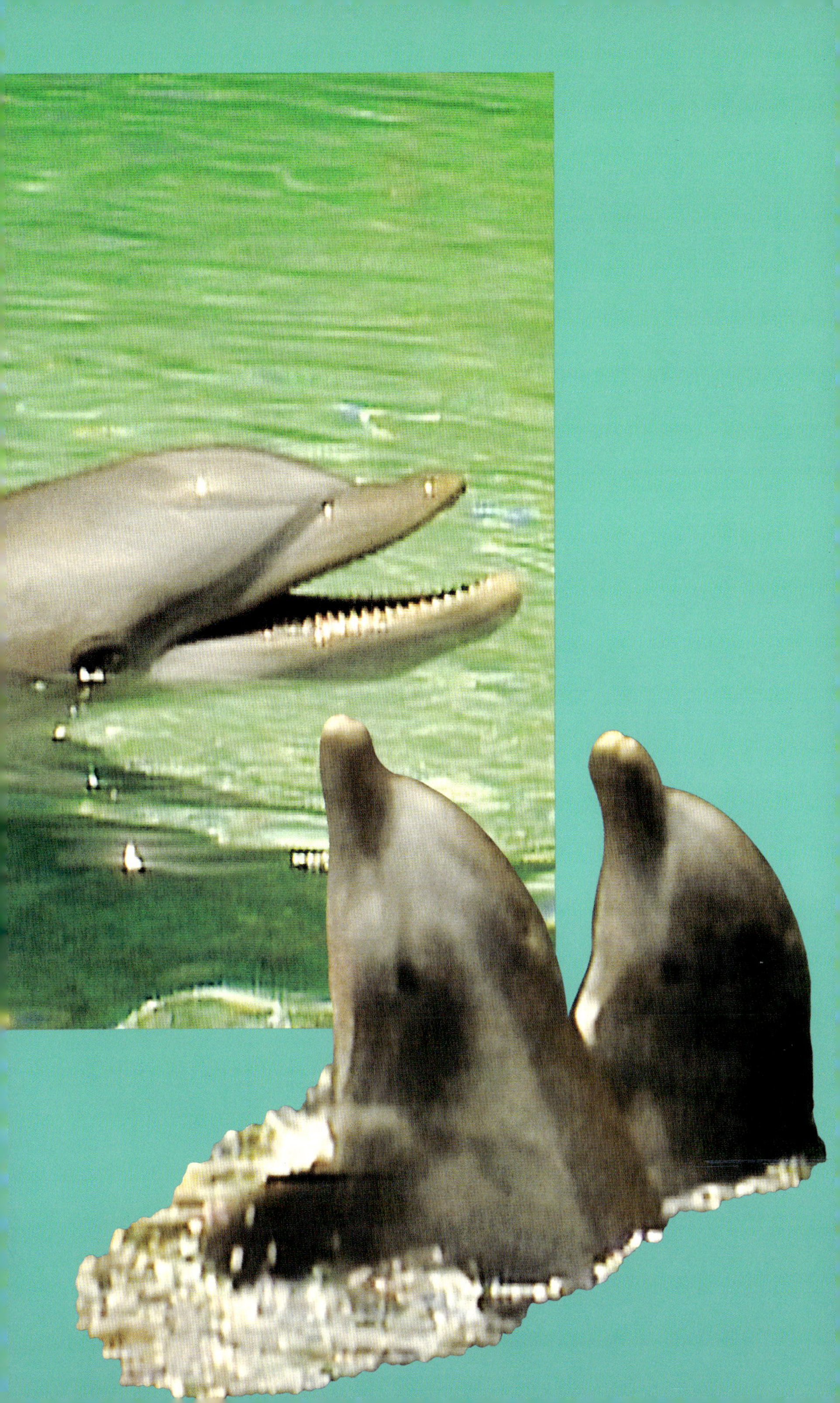

A dolphin leaps in over the linked arms of Renee and Mario. Look at that form!

through the brush or use machetes to hack away vines. That's because the towering rain forest trees filter out most of the sunlight before it reaches the forest floor, resulting in fewer plants at ground level.

Rain forests are made up of many different layers, or as Paul called it, a "multilayered canopy." Each layer has its own distinct community of plants and animals.

From the top of one ancient tree to the top of another ancient tree to the top of still another ancient tree is the upper-level canopy. The top layer of a rain forest can reach two hundred feet in height. That's as tall as a skyscraper! The branches and leaves of these large trees touch one another and act as an umbrella for the lower parts of the rain forest, protecting them from intense sun, heavy rains, and strong winds. The upper-level canopy also prevents sunlight from reaching the floor and keeps the lower layers of the rain forest moist.

Here and there, a few trees grow to heights of 200 to 250 feet. They share space in the temperate rain forest with hemlocks and cedars, but stretch high above the rest of the trees. These giant trees are called "emergents" and they look like slender columns reaching toward the sky, the way a basketball star would look standing in a crowd of regular-sized people. Emergents

ENVIRONMENT

have to be strong in order to survive exposure to the wind and rain above the canopy.

Many rain forest animals live in the upper-level canopy region, because most of the seeds and leaves they feed on grow there. Temperate rain forest canopy dwellers like the red tree vole depend mainly on tree needles for food, shelter, and water. The northern flying squirrel prefers seeds, but adapts to the canopy life in winter by surviving on lichens (LI-kns) that grow there.

The second layer of the rain forest is called the midlevel canopy; small trees, vines, shrubs, and ferns grow here. Trees

Why We Need to Save the Rain Forests

PRACTICAL REASONS

1. Tropical rain forests contain more than half of all the plant and animal species in the world. When the rain forests are destroyed, so are the plants and animals. Scientists say this loss of diversity will have serious consequences for the health of our planet.

2. So far, we've only been able to study a mere 10 percent of the plants and animals in the rain forest, and we're quickly losing an overwhelming portion of the rest. Who knows, those plants and animals that we won't be able to study could hold the cure for cancer . . . or AIDS!

3. Destroying rain forests could drastically change—and not for the better—the world's weather patterns. It speeds up global warming, which threatens agriculture and the quality of human, plant, and animal life worldwide.

4. The loss of thousands of acres of rain forests is already causing problems for the surrounding areas, including increased soil erosion and water pollution. As deforestation continues, these problems will only get worse.

INSPIRATIONAL REASONS

Rain forests are exotic and unique wild places where amazing and strange plants and animals live: They've inspired artists, musicians, and scientists for centuries.

ANIMAL RIGHTS REASONS

Many animal species around the world depend on the rain forests for survival. When their habitats disappear, they become homeless.

HUMAN RIGHTS REASONS

As native rain forest peoples die or are forced to move, the world loses the knowledge of rain forest plants and animals that took these indigenous (in-DIJ-eh-nus) peoples hundreds of years to gather. This info could help scientists develop new crops, medicines, and other vital products.

Indigenous peoples have a right to live where and how they want.

AND FINALLY . . .

People don't have the right to destroy the world's rain forests and other habitats for their own purposes.

ENVIRONMENT

here max out at a height of 80 to 150 feet. This area is home to many different species of birds, including pileated woodpeckers, nuthatches, and warblers.

In the midlevel canopy, sunlight is diffused and winds are reduced to a whisper. The plants that live here get little light and water—only what filters down through the upper-level canopy. Even during the worst thunderstorms, midlevel plants don't always get soaked. But some of the trees in the midlevel canopy are actually waiting to take the places of larger trees in the upper-level canopy.

When a tree dies and falls to the rain forest floor, sunlight finally gets a chance to make its way down to the smaller trees. These trees reach for the sun, grow, and fill in the open space in the upper-level canopy. It can take up to ten years for the midlevel canopy tree to reach upper-level canopy

Thirty-Story Trees!

South and east of the Pacific Northwest rain forests is the home of the world's tallest trees—the redwoods. These giants may live two thousand years and reach 330 feet in height. The record is 368 feet—which is about the size of a thirty-story building! And this tree is only six hundred years old. Think how big it will be when it turns one thousand!

height, but within forty years, the gap will be hard to detect.

The lower-level canopy is occupied by young trees and shrubs that only reach thirty feet. Closer to the ground there are herbs and seedlings. Deer, rabbits, and other temperate rain forest animals get their food here.

The lowest level of the rain forest is the floor. Because of all the trees, only 2 percent of the sunlight ever reaches here, and plant growth is rather limited. But because of the damp and the darkness, it's the perfect environment for all kinds of fungi—like mushrooms—to grow. Some of these "funky fungi" are umbrella shaped; others glow in the dark!

Another thing that you will find on the floor of a rain forest is a nurse log. Nurse logs are trees that have fallen from their place in the canopy. These dead trees continue to generate life, serving as nurseries to tiny hemlock and spruce seedlings. As the logs rot away into the ground, seedlings feed on the nutrients inside. These seedlings will one day take their respective places in the rain forest's multilayered canopy. Elise spotted a young spruce and a western hemlock growing out of the nurse log she found. When the nurse log supporting these trees decays, there will be a soldierlike row of young trees left growing.

ENVIRONMENT

There are also plants that make their homes on the living trees of the rain forest. Mosses, ferns, orchids, and lichens grow on the trunks and branches of trees. They are called "epiphytes" (EH-pe-fites), or air plants. Their human equivalent would be "moochers"—you know, like friends who always ask for a ride, but never give you money for gas! These "moochers" grow on other plants and obtain all their nutrients from the water and dead plant matter that falls on them from the canopy; they do not harm the plants they live on.

The big-leaf maple and the alder can support up to one hundred pounds of mosses and epiphytes (that's like having a seventh-grader tied to your back all the time!). But alders and maples have adapted to these freeloaders and can even send out roots from their own branches to gather nutrients that accumulate in the epiphytes.

WILD, WILD LIFE

The temperate rain forests are home to many different types of freely roaming animals. Caribou and musk oxen thrive on a diet of lichens and mosses. Grizzly and black bears are also common. Snowshoe hares are the favorite dinner of the bobcat, but wolves will eat whatever they can catch—from young or weak caribou and deer, to field mice, and even—pee-yoo—the skunk.

Rain Forests

The most ferocious predator is the wolverine. He's the largest member of the weasel family—twenty-four to forty pounds—but don't let his relation to cuter species fool you. The wolverine has been known to attack even a moose, which stands six feet tall.

Eagles are the keenest hunters of the bird family, and each rain forest has its own specific species. All sit atop the emergent trees, where they can keep an eye on the other animals in the canopy—and check out which ones look good for lunch! The bald eagle lives in the rain forests of the Pacific Northwest and snacks on a variety of animals such as martens, Douglas squirrels, and field

Rain Forest Primer

Who Decided to Call It a Rain Forest, Anyway?
The word "rain forest" was first coined in 1898 by a German botanist to describe forests that grow in constantly wet conditions, or wherever the annual rainfall is more than 80 inches.

Where Can I Find a Rain Forest?
Although rain forests grow in more than fifty countries, about half the total rain forests in the world are contained in Brazil, Zaire (in Africa), and Indonesia.

What's an Ecosystem?
It's a system made up of a community of animals, plants, and bacteria and its interrelated physical and chemical environment.

What's Indigenous?
It means "occurring naturally in a certain area." In terms of the rain forest, "indigenous people" means tribal people—like Native Americans who lived in an area before Europeans arrived. Rain forests are home to 200 million indigenous people.

What Tropical Rain Forest Products Have You Purchased?

You probably aren't aware of it, but there are many different tropical rain forest products in your home right now! Check out your kitchen cupboard. Many spices find their origin in rain forests. Allspice, black pepper, cardamom, chili, cinnamon, cloves, ginger, nutmeg, and sugar are all farmed without harm to the tropical rain forests. The coffee and tea your parents drink and the chocolate used in everything from candy bars to cocoa find their origin in tropical rain forests, too.

A wide variety of fruits and nuts also come from tropical rain forests, such as oranges, bananas, avocados, coconuts, grapefruits, lemons, limes, tangerines, pineapples, and mangoes. Some fruits and flowers are even used to produce different oils for perfumes. Did you know that chewing gum comes from resin in the rubber trees? While some of these products can be farmed outside tropical rain forests, others cannot.

ENVIRONMENT

mice. The monkey-eating eagle of the Asian rain forest has a heartier appetite and likes to prey on unsuspecting primates!

Over 80 million insect species live in rain forests and are a very vital part of rain forest ecosystems. Insects feed on the dead leaves and animal waste that fall from above, sort of like rain forest recyclers. Each year termites process up to one ton of leaf litter from each acre of the rain forest floor.

With such an abudance of animals in the rain forest, you'd expect to see wildlife everywhere you look, but it's not always that easy. Many animals blend into their surroundings as a means of protection, whether they're the hunted or the hunter.

But others have colors and patterns that make them more conspicuous. Many of these animals, such as the strawberry poison dart frogs, are toxic. Others taste bad, or sting. Their coloring warns predators to leave them alone. Some harmless species have similar color patterns to trick predators. For example, the scarlet king snake looks just like the poisonous coral snake. It's not poisonous, but who wants to check?

VARIETY IS THE SPICE OF LIFE

Why should I be concerned about the rain forests when I live in Ohio? you ask. After all, there's nothing in it for me. Or is there?

Each species of plants and animals is unique, different from every other species. This "biological diversity," or variety, is very important to humans. In other words, our survival depends on the survival of other species. When a species is lost, any benefits it might have provided to people are lost also. Perhaps it produces a chemical that could be used as a medicine—almost half of all the medicines we use are derived from rain forest plants and animals. There are at least one thousand known plant species that are used to combat cancer. Tamoxifen, for instance, which is found in old-growth yew trees, has been used in the fight against breast cancer.

ENVIRONMENT

There are many other plants that are used to make stimulants, sedatives, and antibiotics. Some tropical vines are used to make a muscle relaxant used during surgery. Certain frogs even produce a substance that is used as a local anesthetic, a muscle relaxer, and a painkiller. Although these frogs may not be princes in disguise, they are making people feel like royalty.

There are also wild varieties of domesticated crops with features that could improve the crop. The future of our food supply depends on improving domestic crops by breeding them with these related wild plants. Other rain forest plants produce chemical compounds that can be used as pesticides. Who knows? One day, maybe rain forest plants will even be used as a source of fuel.

While some of these chemical compounds are now being produced synthetically, many still have to be obtained from the plant or animal itself. Soon this may not be possible, however, since scientists estimate that one to six species, mostly plants and insects, are lost forever each hour.

WHERE DID ALL THE TREES GO?

When our adventurers came across a field of freshly planted seedlings, they saw firsthand the efforts to rebuild temperate rain forests after the devastation of "clear-cut logging"—a forest management practice that involves cutting all the trees within an area at one time. The forest area Jordan and Elise saw had been quickly and completely cleared by the chain saws, skidders, and bulldozers of the loggers. The burned remains of old-growth trees stuck up through the soil and most everything was black. Little trees were then planted where the mighty forest once stood. But it will take at least sixty years for the forest to return to the way it was.

Unfortunately, this scenario isn't uncommon in the Pacific Northwest. Miles and miles of national parks are this way, where deals are made to sell off the state-run temperate rain forests to commercial loggers. A brochure from the Washington Department of Natural Resources claims that the logged areas are giving birth to a "new generation of forest."

But what the brochure doesn't say is that clear-cutting a forest destroys not only the forest, but also its vital biodiversity. The loggers come in and cut everything in sight—from Western hemlocks, Sitka spruce, and Douglas firs to maples, oaks, and hickories. Sure the Forest Service replants, but only with a few species valued by the timber industry. Gone forever are many ancient trees that are necessary to life in the temperate rain forest.

Amazing Rain Forest Facts

Some things you eat that come from rain forests are oranges, bananas, grapefruit, sweet potatoes, and chewing gum.

A common medicine that comes from rain forests is ipecac, which is used to reverse the effects of possible poisoning by inducing vomiting. (If you accidentally ate poison berries when you were a kid, your mom probably gave you ipecac.)

Animals of the rain forest include a bird called the cassowary, a ferocious flightless bird native to New Guinea. It stands close to six feet tall and runs like the wind. You wouldn't want to meet up with it: The cassowary has legs strong enough to rip open a human belly with one swipe!

The tiniest known primate (humans and monkeys are primates also) lives in the rain forest, too. It is the hairy-eared dwarf lemur, which measures five inches in length, not counting its furry seven-inch tail. This tiny animal only weighs three and a half ounces! It was recently found in the last remaining soggy rain forest of Madagascar and is the only surviving species of a whole genus of lemurs.

All domestic chickens—including the one used in the McNuggets you had for lunch—are direct descendants of four species of Asian rain forest fowl.

It only takes a single minute to destroy a section of tropical rain forest the size of ten city blocks!

A four-ounce hamburger made from rain forest beef involves the destruction of about fifty-five square feet

Rain Forests

of tropical forest—an area the size of a small kitchen. Disposable chopsticks are often made from tropical timber. In 1979, Japan alone used enough wood in its disposable chopsticks to make eleven thousand family-sized timber-framed homes. Much of this wood came from tropical rain forests.

Bats that live in the rain forest are the most important seed-dispersing animals in the world. They contribute 95 percent of the seed dispersal that leads to reforestation.

You can actually "adopt an acre" of rain forest, which buys protection of specific areas of threatened rain forest. For information, write to: Adopt-an-Acre Program, The Nature Conservancy, 1815 North Lynn Street, Arlington, VA 22209.

A "managed" forest grown and regrown on clear-cut land is not a natural forest. It is never given time to regenerate its original biodiversity. No one knows for sure if these forests can be "managed" for more than a few years before completely dying out. And each day approximately 170 acres of old-growth trees are destroyed. At the present rate of cutting, the original forests will all be gone in fourteen years. Could the "managed" forest be far behind?

The uncontrolled pace of cutting of the old-growth forests has caused great concern and debate among citizens, the U.S. Forest Service, which owns most of the

ENVIRONMENT

remaining old-growth forests, and commercial loggers. The Forest Service tries to hide its work from the public by leaving narrow strips of tall trees by highways to hide the destruction. But they can't hide the acres of naked land.

Citizens are enraged at the speed at which the temperate rain forests in the Pacific Northwest are vanishing. The law states that the Forest Service is not allowed to cut a forest any faster than a secondary forest can replace it. However, the Forest Service is cutting 25 percent faster than that. All totaled, the Forest Service has logging operations in 160 forests, selling seventy thousand acres of old-growth forest a year. Soon they'll have to figure out if it's possible to carry on such massive logging *and* protect the wilderness areas *and* promote hiking, hunting, and other recreational activities in the national parks.

The loggers aren't concerned with biodiversity, however, *or* Pacific Northwest vacationers. They feel their jobs are more important than the health of the Pacific Northwest's rain forests. Entire communities in the Pacific Northwest depend on logging for employment and financial support. Restaurants and shops hang signs stating that "logging dollars support this establishment." Without the timber industry, people would be without work, homes, and food, much like the animals of the rain forests the loggers destroy. It is a growing problem, without an easy answer.

SPOTTED OWL CONTROVERSY

Amid all this controversy, a rather reluctant star has emerged—the shy northern spotted owl—not through its own doing, but because of the battle United States environmentalists are waging to save its home in the temperate rain forests of the Pacific Northwest.

Over the past century, the U.S. Forest Service has allowed timber companies to cut down large amounts of ancient trees—80 percent, in fact—from national forests. These trees were home to the northern spotted owl, and it is this clear-cut activity that has led to the critical decline in the spotted owl population. When the National Audubon Society finally estimated that only 2,600 pairs of the birds remained in the entire Pacific Northwest, they put pressure on the U.S. Fish and Wildlife Service to list the northern spotted owl as a threatened species. This requires the government to create a plan to curb logging and provide protection for the bird. But this won't bring back the owls that have already died or guarantee that logging restrictions will stay intact. And as Paul pointed out, the northern spotted owls are merely an "indicator species." They remind us that as their population drops off, the health of our forests and of all the animals that live with the owls is dropping off, too.

SPEAKING OUT FOR THE TREES

Some researchers estimate that fifty acres of rain forest are destroyed each minute; others say it's closer to one hundred. Imagine if a city simply vanished, leaving the people who lived there without homes. That's exactly what's happening to the plants and animals in the rain forest. By the year 2034, half of all the existing rain forests could be gone.

Such disregard for rain forests and their communities is what fuels environmental groups such as Earth First! This group's slogan is "No compromise in defense of Mother Earth." The organization was among the first environmental groups to try and save the old-growth forests. At rallies and demonstrations, members have dressed as trees and spotted owls. They have held sit-ins at logging sites, linking arms to prevent—at least for a while—the cutting of five-hundred-year-old trees.

Some of the efforts of Earth First!, however, have not been considered admirable. Some of their tactics have included pouring sand in fuel tanks of logging equipment and driving metal spikes into trees. These spikes ruin the chain saws used by loggers. Other environmental groups fear that these tactics hurt rather than help the environmental cause and scare off potential supporters. But the Earth First! people feel their actions draw much-needed attention to such issues as saving the Pacific Northwest rain forests.

Believe it or not, there are some rain forests where humans, plants, and animals do live in harmony. Tropical rain forests still provide homes for many tribes of indigenous people. Each rain forest tribe has a culture that is closely tied to the environment in which it lives. Many continue to live in a traditional manner, relying on rain forest plants and animals to supply them with most of their needs. They continue to live as hunters, farmers, and fishermen and gather over one hundred species of plants to use for tools, furniture, baskets, dyes, and medicines. They also sell fruits, nuts, fish, and meat to buyers outside the rain forest. But unlike most Americans, the Amazon people understand the importance of taking from the rain forest without harming it.

HOW CAN I HELP?

The forces destroying rain forests can't be stopped overnight, but there are reasons to be hopeful. All around the world, people are starting to take action, but everyone needs to do his part—even you! Quite possibly the easiest way to help save the environment is by

Portrait of an Indigenous People: The Efe

On the other side of the world, deep in the heart of the Congo River basin in Zaire, Africa, lies the Ituri Forest. It is a tropical rain forest. Among the many tribes living there is a group called the Efe (pronounced EH-fay). They live very differently from most of us and exist in harmony with the rain forest. There's a lot we can learn from them.

The Efe are pygmies. Typically, they have reddish brown skin and are short, rarely growing to be more than four and one-half feet tall. Some indigenous peoples are farmers, some are hunter-gatherers; the Efe fall into the latter group. They forage for food in the wild (as opposed to growing their own), taking advantage of whatever the forest has to offer. They hunt with spears, blowguns, and bows and arrows, catching game in traps, nets, or snares. Their dietary staples include antelope (called duikers), monkeys, rodents, birds, and honey.

The Efe live in communities made up of small bands of several families. While everyone shares chores, the men generally hunt and collect honey (which accounts for a major portion of their total yearly calorie intake), while the women fish, build huts, collect wood and water, prepare food, and care for the children.

The forest shelters the Efe from nature's elements. It also provides materials for their homes, which are huts made from trees and covered with leaves. And it provides their clothing—they actually hammer tree bark into cloth. Although the Efe use the rain forest for survival, they don't hurt it the way outsiders do. Many Efe bands migrate from site to site. Their numbers are small, and they take only what they need to survive.

recycling, which we talked about in the recycling chapter (page 58). If we recycle paper, the demand for both temperate and tropical rain forest timber is reduced.

Elise showed Jordan and *Name Your Adventure* viewers another way to counter the decrease in rain forest trees when she planted a western red cedar seedling (which Jordan preferred to call Bertha). When forests are replanted, special attention must be given to diversity. Rain forests are made up of many different species. Loggers who plant managed forests tend to replant with one species of tree, arranging them in neat rows close together. If an insect or plant disease then attacks one tree, the next thing you know, the entire managed forest is gone.

In a natural forest, adequate spacing among trees of the same species is protection against this type of loss. That's why foresters, and even many loggers, are copying the ways of the natural forest when they replant. Instead of concentrating on only one or two species, they try to make these managed forests as diverse as possible. Then they leave the area alone to renew itself.

Want to know even more ways to get involved? How about putting up a bird feeder in your backyard? Many North American songbirds actually migrate from the Central and South American rain forests. Your bird-

ENVIRONMENT

seed provides them with food on their long flight—and helps save a rain forest species!

Even something as simple as shopping can help save the rain forest. When you go to the store, make sure you make a special effort to buy foods that support the rain forest. Some companies make products that are harvested from rain forest materials, but don't threaten the rain forest's survival. Ben & Jerry's Homemade Ice Cream makes Rainforest Crunch candy and ice cream using Brazil nuts bought from the Amazon people—now you've got a good environmental reason to pig out!

You can become an activist and help stop the destruction without going to extremes—just spread the message to your friends and family. Ask your teacher to devote class time to talking about our rain forests. Maybe she could run a special program with a rain forest theme, like an essay or poster contest, a letter-writing campaign asking politicians to support laws that will help protect rain forests, or a display of rain forest products used or manufactured in your area.

Still not enough? Well, you can even adopt an acre of rain forest through the Nature Conservancy Adopt-an-Acre Program or the World Wildlife Fund. For your donation, you'll receive an honorary land deed, and all funds support the acquisition of rain forest land.

Rain Forests

Rain forests have been forever changed by humans. We can only wonder what some of the original forest might have looked like or how tall the tallest Douglas fir in the Pacific Northwest was. As Paul pointed out to Jordan and Elise, "In our ancient forests, we have a library of information. We're just learning how it all functions."

Elise realizes that we can all do our part in saving the environment by using the earth's forest resources wisely. Let's hope everyone else does, too. Then maybe rain forests, including the one *Name Your Adventure* jetted off to, will still be around to enjoy in the future.

Dolphins—Encounter of the Closest Kind

"Beautiful, intelligent, and lovable." Is Mario describing the girl of his dreams? No! He's describing dolphins, some of the smartest mammals on the planet. And Mario should know what he's talking about; he actually got to swim with dolphins at the Dolphin Quest facility when he traveled to Hawaii with seventeen-year-old Renee Gragnano to meet our flippered friends.

Here, people learn how important it is to protect these creatures as they observe the natural behavior of dolphins in the wild.

Before swimming with the dolphins, Mario and Renee had to take a class to learn what to expect. Then Jill from Dolphin Quest helped them prepare for their dolphin encounter. When they were ready, Mario and Renee slipped on life vests and prepared to meet their two dolphin friends.

Mario and Renee dove right in to swim with the dolphins. But neither of them first established contact.

It's the dolphins who get to choose how much interaction swimmers will have. And it was the dolphins who ultimately decided if Mario or Renee would even get to touch them.

Renee was pretty excited to be on the big island of Hawaii, but not as excited as she was to swim with the dolphins. Renee's interest in dolphins began when she was five years old and her mother took her to Marineland in California for the first time. When she saw the dolphin show, she wanted to jump right in. And she's been fascinated with dolphins ever since.

At a marine park like Marineland, people get to learn even more about these magnificent mammals as they perform a series of activities in a show. Watching the dolphins interact with their trainers is a special sight. Who could help wanting to jump in the pool and take part in these activities, too?

Dolphin training is actually a relatively new field. People first started working with marine mammals in captivity only about thirty years ago. Marineland in St. Augustine, Florida, was the first park to have dolphins housed in pools perform for an audience. Things have changed since then, and as humans have continued to work with dolphins, we have kept learning more and more about these unique creatures.

When Is a Fish Not a Fish? . . . When It's a Dolphin!

You find them in the seas and oceans. They have fins and flippers and gills. They glide through the water effortlessly. Must be some kind of fish, right? Not if it's a dolphin! Although many people assume they're just another species of fish, dolphins—as well as whales, porpoises, and dugongs—are actually mammals, just like apes, monkeys, and . . . humans!

A fish, by scientific definition, is a cold-blooded, water-dwelling animal with a backbone and skeleton. It breathes oxygen from the water through gills and has a mouth full of teeth.

A mammal is a warm-blooded vertebrate animal with a backbone and skeleton. Females have mammary glands which are used to feed their young.

Dolphins are warm-blooded, air-breathing mammals.

ENVIRONMENT

SO YOU WANT TO BE A DOLPHIN TRAINER?

An interest in psychology is a must for any would-be dolphin specialist. You need at least two years of college, although a four-year degree in psychology would even be better; marine parks specifically look for trainers who have degrees in psychology. Studying psychology is so important because dolphin trainers deal with behavior modification day in and day out. It doesn't hurt to have some training in marine biology or zoology, either.

Obviously, a dolphin trainer has to know how to swim—well! You'll also need your scuba certification. That's because when trainers aren't working and playing with the dolphins, they have to help clean and maintain the pools.

Being in great physical condition is a must, as well, because training dolphins is a very physical job. It's strenuous business doing all those shows and training sessions, and working with all those dolphins.

There are over thirty different kinds of dolphin. Most marine parks have bottle-nosed dolphins, which get their name from the shape of their mouth. The Pacific white-sided dolphin is becoming popular in some parks, too. These dolphins actually resemble the killer whale, with their beautiful black-and-white coloring.

Dolphins range from six to thirteen feet in length, and an adult can weigh between two hundred and four hundred pounds. The two dolphins Mario and Renee got to play with were eight feet in length and weighed a whopping four hundred pounds apiece. They were also both males, which, like humans, tend to be bigger than the females.

Both in the wild and in captivity, most dolphins live to be thirty to thirty-five years old. But there's no such thing as a retirement home for dolphins in captivity; they continue to perform even in old age. Sea World in San Diego, California, has a dolphin named Corky that's thirty years old and still performing—simply because she loves to do it.

ENVIRONMENT

LET'S GO TO DOLPHIN SCHOOL

Whether in the wild or in captivity, dolphins have certain behaviors that are "instinctual." That means they do these things naturally, like swimming, breathing, and eating.

Trainers use these instinctual behaviors to help them teach the dolphins new "learned behaviors," like taking a bow. That's where the dolphin jumps out of the water and arches its back. Dolphins can easily jump twenty feet in the air—some can even jump as high as forty to fifty feet! Other examples of learned behaviors include back dives, where the dolphin jumps out of the water and does a back dive; the tail walk, where the dolphin moves along the water on its tail; a fluke wave, where the dolphin waves to the audience with its fluke (a fluke is another name for the dolphin's tail); a spin swim, where the dolphin spins its body while it swims around the tank; and the fast swim, where the dolphin swims around the pool really fast. Dolphins are one of the fastest swimmers, reaching speeds of twenty-five to thirty miles per hour.

Sometimes dolphins will even use their bodies to communicate. They may jump out of the water and land on their side. This is called a side breach. They may slap their pectoral flippers or their flukes on the water. They may even clap their jaws together and make noisy splashes.

Once again, the trainer takes note of all these behaviors and incorporates them into the training process by moving his or her body to correspond with the dolphin's movement. The trainer may point to a certain area of the pool where the dolphin is to swim, using his or her body as a signal. Or the trainer could turn around in a circle while in the water, encouraging the dolphin to perform the exact same behavior.

Then there's the human hurdle, where the dolphin jumps over the trainer while he or she is in the water. When Mario and Renee were at Dolphin Quest, a dolphin jumped right over *them*! You've probably even seen some of these "tricks" when you visited a marine park or aquarium.

Most behaviors dolphins do at marine parks are actually things they

Dolphins Do Good

Swimming with dolphins is a fascinating experience for most people. But for disabled and handicapped people, it is a life-enhancing and educational experience. The Dolphin Research Center runs an ongoing dolphin/child program that has helped many disabled children learn by working with dolphins. Therapy sessions include working on motor skills and coordination, lengthening attention spans, or even alleviating depression.

ENVIRONMENT

would do on their own in the wild from time to time, as when a dolphin starts jumping, squirting, or breaching. Breaching is when a dolphin jumps out of the water, lands, and makes an enormous splash.

Trainers take these natural behaviors one step further and teach the dolphin to perform them on cue. This is done through "operant conditioning," a type of learning that changes behaviors through the rewards that follow. When a dolphin performs a behavior that's close to what the trainer wants, the trainer will give it a reward, or "positive reinforcement." This can be anything that is pleasing to the animal. Food is a positive reinforcement, but it only really works if the dolphin is hungry, so trainers have to rely on other reinforcements as well.

If a dolphin breaches

Dolphins Swim with the Sharks—and Outsmart 'Em!

When threatened by an animal of greater strength and size—say a large shark—a group of dolphins will suddenly band tightly together. They'll all dive below the shark and drive their blunt noses into the predator's belly, one after another. The shark, who thought he had a free lunch, is defeated by the intelligence of the dolphins, who instinctively join together to save themselves.

on command and gets one of its favorite reinforcements, chances are that it will soon *want* to breach on command. We learn in the same way. It doesn't take us long to figure out that we can watch hours of hunky Mario and *Name Your Adventure* videotapes as soon as we get our homework done.

The problem is that dolphins can't always tell their trainers what they like, so the trainers have to watch the dolphins closely to see what their reactions are to different reinforcements. Across the board, trainers have found that touch is an incredibly strong reinforcement. That's because the dolphin's skin, which feels like a hard-boiled egg without the shell, is much more sensitive than human skin. Mario thinks petting a dolphin is a lot like touching a little baby because its skin is so soft. What's more, it's not really flaky like ours, but sloughs off when the dolphins rub their bodies against the sides of their pools.

By observing the dolphins rubbing certain parts of their bodies against the tank, trainers have learned that being touched is pleasing to the dolphin. Trainers can spend thirty minutes giving a dolphin a body rub, and the dolphin still wants more! Mario and Renee found out that their two dolphin friends loved nuzzling and cuddling, and being tickled under the chin.

Other reinforcements include having their tongues

ENVIRONMENT

scratched, getting squirted with a hose, and playing with toys.

Of course, nobody's perfect, and sometimes dolphins don't always do exactly what the trainers want. That's okay, they still receive positive reinforcement! There's simply no negativity or punishment in their world, at least as far as training goes. Just imagine if you were a dolphin: You wouldn't get sent to bed without dinner if you forgot to do your chores!

Still, the reinforcement for bad behavior isn't anything great like a bucket of fish. It's called LRS, the "least reinforcing stimulus." If a dolphin's been goofing around instead of fluke waving, for instance, its trainer will simply stand perfectly still for three seconds. Her body language tells the dolphin, "Okay, you didn't do it quite right, but that's all right." Then the trainer will either ask the dolphin to try the behavior again or skip it and go on to something else.

A positive reinforcement lets the dolphin know that it's done the behavior correctly. And it's important to let the dolphin know right away because a lapse of even a few seconds could reinforce the wrong behavior. Unfortunately, it's not always possible to reinforce a dolphin during a performance, so the trainer uses signals to let the dolphins know that they've done the right thing. This is called a bridge signal, and it's usually a special whistle.

Since dolphins talk to one another in squeaks, whistles, and chirps, the whistle actually lets the trainer talk to the dolphin in its own language. The trainers use a whistle that sounds at the dolphin's own natural frequency, so the dolphin has no problem hearing it, even underwater. Humans in the audience, however, usually can't hear it at all.

Trainers have also begun to use underwater sounds, or tones, played through underwater speakers. This is a relatively new technique in which groups of computer codes are organized to represent each animal's name and some simple words. Dolphins are taught to respond to these sounds as well. And like the whistle, most humans can't hear these tones.

TRAINING SESSIONS

So far we've talked about reinforcement and communication. Now let's put it all together and see how a captive dolphin is trained to jump up and touch a target on command.

First, the behavior is broken down into smaller steps. The trainer may use his hand or a target like a long pole for the dolphin to focus on. Step one: The trainer touches the target to the dolphin's nose, sounding the whistle and reinforcing the animal with a fish or a back rub. This gets repeated several times.

ENVIRONMENT

Then, when the dolphin starts connecting rewards with touching the target, the pole is moved a couple of inches away. Then a foot away, then two feet away, and so on. Every time the dolphin touches the target, the whistle is sounded, and the reinforcement is given.

But how do trainers get dolphins to interact with them in the first place? They start out by building a friendship. This means spending a lot of time touching, rubbing, and playing together in the water. The trainers want to make sure that the dolphins enjoy being with them. Then they gradually start to teach them different behaviors.

Training schedules vary throughout the week, but the most important sessions are always the one-on-ones, which build trusting relationships between trainer and dolphin. It's important to make each training session different because it's variety that keeps the dolphins mentally stimulated. It keeps them thinking, What do I get to do next? Who's going to be doing it? Which pool are we going to be in?

Even the performances are carefully designed so the dolphins can't guess what's going to happen next. That's when you run into trouble. . . .

It would be as if you went to math class every day and had to solve the same problem every time. You'd eventually think, I'm not going to class today. I'm not

DOLPHINS

going this week. I'm not going this week. I'm not going this month. And that's pretty much what dolphins think, too, when they get bored with their routines. That's why trainers try so hard to make every day different.

DOLPHIN AEROBICS

Besides teaching the dolphins different behaviors, trainers also make sure that the dolphins stay in shape. These underwater gymnasts need to be in good physical condition, but there's no such thing as a dolphin aerobics class! Their sessions consist of different activities that are fun for dolphins. Sometimes the trainer jumps in and out of the water with the dolphins. Other times, the trainers will run back and forth from pool to pool and

Baby Dolphin Facts

1. Dolphin babies are called calves.
2. Bottle-nosed dolphin calves weigh between thirty and forty pounds at birth.
3. Dolphin moms nurse their calves just like humans do.
4. A baby dolphin rolls its tongue around Mom's nipple to help keep the salt water out. The edges of its tongue are fringed and will seal almost like a zipper.
5. Babies swim in the echelon position, a bit behind and to the side of Mom, so that they will be towed along in her wake.
6. Sometimes another dolphin will act as a midwife during birth to help the baby take its first breath, or act as a babysitter later on.
7. Dolphin calves are born with a few hairs on their rostrum (snout), but these soon fall out.

have the dolphins follow. The goal is to gradually lengthen the amount of time that the dolphins are moving, thereby building their stamina.

The dolphins need to be able to perform a demanding half-hour show several times a day, but the first time that a dolphin exercises, it's not going to be a full thirty minutes. Imagine how you'd feel if you pumped iron for thirty minutes straight on the first day of a new exercise program!

Of course, just like people, sometimes dolphins don't want to go to work—but unlike people, captive dolphins get their way! If they don't want to participate in a show, it's their choice. They'll get terrific reinforcement if they do choose to perform, but if they'd rather take a breather, then they just receive LRS.

During one audience volunteer sequence at Sea World in Orlando, Florida, several years ago, one of the dolphins decided that she wasn't going to work anymore. She just up and left and went to play at the bottom of the pool. Everyone thought the dolphin had called it quits for the day because her departure was so sudden. But then the dolphin resurfaced, opened her mouth, and presented her trainers with a shiny, golden wedding ring!

The retrieval behavior was something the dolphin

had learned in its training sessions, and it certainly deserved a special reward, so the trainer stopped the show, had a big play time with the dolphin just to let her know, "Thank you very much! You did a super job!" But when it was time to go on with the performance, the dolphin disappeared again! Seconds later, she resurfaced with yet another ring! Looks like positive reinforcement has its own rewards!

LIKE MOTHER, LIKE BABY—DOLPHIN!

Trainers aren't the dolphins' only teachers. Like humans, dolphins learn from their parents. But while human babies don't start learning to walk until they're about ten months old, dolphins learn to swim the minute they're born. In fact, they start learning many things right at birth, such as eating and communication, from their mothers, their siblings, and other dolphins in their environment.

Unlike domestic animals like cats and dogs, dolphins don't have to leave their parents when they reach a certain age. They can stay with them for as long as they like. Dolphins are gregarious creatures, which means they enjoy spending time with other dolphins, as well as with people. From time to time, they'll go off and play on their own, or the trainer can work with them individually to teach them to learn things by themselves. But for

ENVIRONMENT

the most part, they would rather be together. Some scientists even believe that if left all alone, a dolphin would die of loneliness.

Once a mother is comfortable with her calf in their environment, she will start allowing people to get closer. It's around this time that she also teaches the little calf to eat pieces of solid food. To do this, she'll break up the baby's fish into small pieces and teach the baby to play with the fish before he or she eats it. That's when the trainers can also start introducing pieces of fish and other reinforcements to the baby dolphin to slowly build their own relationships with the baby.

It's not very long between the time that a trainer starts working with a dolphin and the time that dolphin is performing in the show. Usually, the calf will swim right alongside the mother to begin with, until it feels safe and comfortable. In fact, the baby gets most of its

Where Did the Dolphin Come From?

The dolphin is a descendant of a sea creature that once lived on the land. For some unknown reason, this creature returned to the sea millions of years ago. What were once their forelegs have been modified into flippers that are now used for steering. Their hind legs have disappeared entirely.

introduction to performing by following Mom and doing just what she does.

A DAY IN THE LIFE OF A DOLPHIN TRAINER

There's no typical day in the life of a dolphin trainer, but there are certain aspects of the job that must be done every day. For instance, trainers have to make sure that they feed the dolphins correctly. A dolphin eats about thirty pounds of fish a day, including smelt, herring, and squid. Each dolphin gets the same amount of food every day no matter what.

Dolphins don't get to pig out on all their food at once, though. Just as in their training, feeding sessions vary, plus they get treats as reinforcers. Sometimes there are two or three feeding sessions, sometimes six or seven. It's always different. The more variety dolphins get, the happier they are.

To keep things from being predictable in both the training and feeding sessions, the dolphins get to work with all the different trainers—anywhere from five to eight at any one park. (This also allows hardworking trainers days off now and then!)

Besides working with trainers, dolphins need to learn to interact with veterinarians, too. About once a week, each dolphin receives a routine vet check to monitor its health and growth. The trainers teach them cer-

ENVIRONMENT

tain behaviors that will make these exams a little bit easier for everyone. For example, the dolphins learn to lie on their backs and place their flukes at the side of the pool so the vet can get a blood sample. Mario and Renee saw this move firsthand. Blood is taken from a vein in the fluke about once a month, just to check on the dolphin's general health. Once a vet knows what a dolphin's healthy blood is like, he or she can easily spot any changes that might mean sickness or infection.

After the blood has been taken, a positive reinforcement is given. Think back to a time when you had to go to the doctor and have a sample of your blood taken. It wasn't much fun, was it? But if you got to go out for pizza or ice cream afterward, it made it a little better in the long run. That's what a positive reinforcement does for the dolphin, too.

In addition to the blood sample, the dolphins are also taught how to urinate on command so the vet can take a urine sample. This helps the vet find other signs of infection or tell if a female is pregnant. Several other behaviors also help with medical procedures, like opening their blowhole and taking a breath on command. (Dolphins breathe through the blowhole, which is located at the top of their head. They can close their blowhole and remain underwater for up to six minutes.) This helps the vet check their lungs. The doctor does the same thing to you when he places a stethoscope on your back and asks you to inhale and exhale.

Dolphins are even taught how to open their mouths and move their tongues to let the vet check their teeth. Any cavities?

ANIMAL AMBASSADORS

Over the years, millions of visitors to marine parks are not only entertained by dolphins, but they're also educated. Mario and Renee learned a great deal when they visited Dolphin Quest—not only about dolphins, but also about how to help conserve the environment. A few performing dolphins in captivity—"animal ambassadors," if you will—can educate thousands of people, ensuring a higher quality of life for the other dolphins in the wild.

Still, some people don't believe that dolphins, or any other animals, should be kept in captivity. These animal activists feel strongly that all dolphins should be free to swim in the ocean. The trainers understand these activists' feelings and are quick to point out that the captive dolphins are treated extremely well. Unlike dolphins in the ocean, who have to hunt for food constantly, animals in a marine park are fed thirty pounds of fish a day. They never have to go to bed hungry just because the fishing was poor.

Marine parks like Dolphin Quest go to great

Dive Right In and Learn More about It!

Here's How You Can Find Out More about Dolphins

Head to your local library or bookstore and pick up one of the informative and picturesque books about dolphins. One of the newest is called "The Lives of Dolphins and Whales," by Richard C. Connor and Dawn M. Peterson.

Join one of the two excellent not-for-profit organizations dedicated to dolphin education and preservation. One is the Center for Marine Conservation, at 1725 DeSales Street N.W., Washington, DC 20036. This organization fights to protect all endangered marine wildlife. The other is called the Dolphin Research Center, and can be reached by writing to P.O. Box 522875, Marathon Shores, FL 33052-2875. It is dedicated to "a better understanding of marine mammals and the environment we share." Both organizations send out newsletters.

"Adopt a Dolphin" is a program run by the Dolphin Research Center in which you become a "dolphin parent." You receive a certificate of adoption with your name, the dolphin's name and photo, T-shirts, and other small gifts. Your dollars go toward supporting work done at the Dolphin Research Center.

Swim with the dolphins, as Mario and our adventurer did. This, however, is easier said than done. Within the United States, there are four heavily regulated SWTD programs. The Dolphin Research Center runs one called Dolphin Encounter. There are two other programs, also located in the Florida Keys. The fourth, Dolphin Quest in Hawaii (the one "Name Your Adventure" went to) is open to hotel guests only. All four of the programs book early and you may have to wait more than a year before you actually get to swim.

lengths to provide environments that are very similar to a dolphin's natural habitat. Warm-water dolphins live in comfortably heated pools. Cold-water dolphins get things a little chillier. Pools are also cleaner than oceans and guaranteed free from pollutants, sewage, oil spills, and dumping.

Renee voiced another problem that dolphins in the wild must face when she said, "I just don't think that enough people realize how they are hurting dolphins just by buying tuna that's not dolphin safe."

Because dolphins and tuna often travel together, fishermen use dolphins to help them locate tuna in the Pacific Ocean. Inevitably, dolphins get caught in the huge nets—up to three-quarters of a mile long and six hundred feet deep—which fishermen use to catch tuna. Although the fishermen make efforts to free the dolphins before bringing the tuna on board, millions of dolphins have been killed. The tuna fishermen mean the dolphins no harm; they just have to find better ways of getting them out of the tuna nets and back into the sea alive. And because tuna fishing is big business, no one is ready to give up using nets in exchange for the hook-and-line method just for the sake of the dolphins—unless, of course, people stop buying their tuna! It takes only a second to check the label on the next can of tuna you buy, to make sure it says "Dolphin Safe."

ENVIRONMENT

The fact that the dolphins are interested in learning and interacting with their trainers is one sure sign that they're happy in captivity. But the best indication may be that they're breeding and having healthy babies. Lots of baby dolphins and killer whales have been born in captivity—so many that several marine parks don't even take their animals from the wild anymore. At Sea World, for example, it's been almost twelve years since they took a dolphin or killer whale from the wild; about 70 percent of their dolphins and killer whales were born at one of their four parks.

Nevertheless, the activists still protest. Maybe you even saw them on television news, demanding the release of captive whales and dolphins around the time that *Free Willy* was playing in movie theaters.

It may sound like a nice idea, but could captive animals really make it on their own in the wild? Would they know how to hunt for food or take care of themselves in the ocean? Imagine being raised and cared for in your neighborhood for your entire childhood, and then suddenly being taken to another state, dropped off, and told, "Okay, you're twelve years old now—so long! Go make a living for yourself. Find your own home and food." It wouldn't be easy.

SO YOU WANT TO BE A DOLPHIN TRAINER

Giving a little kindness to animals is exactly what a trainer does. And the dolphins give back kindness in return. Ask any dolphin trainer, and he or she'll tell you there aren't many careers as satisfying as this one. There's no better feeling than when the dolphin responds to your command.

Satisfying, yes, but it's not exactly the most glamorous job. You don't get to dress up—unless you consider a wet suit evening wear. Forget painted nails, makeup, and cologne—nothing will cover the fishy smell you'll get from having your hands in a pail of smelt! And you'll find fish scales in the strangest places, like on your knuckles, in your hair, and on your cheek when quitting time rolls around—if it ever does. Dolphin training can be a round-the-clock job at times. The dolphins depend on you, and their needs come first. They don't know it's your birthday or Christmas. When they need you, you have to be there. It all comes with the territory when you decide to be a dolphin trainer.

Still interested in becoming a trainer? Who wouldn't be? Mario said it best when he had his dolphin encounter of the closest kind: "When you hold one of these guys in your arms, you realize how gentle they really are. And they're so smart and fun. It's like they just want to play and have a good time."

ENVIRONMENT

Dolphins are so lovable and adorable, training them may look like a day at the beach. But it's not quite as easy as jumping in the water and playing with the dolphins. There are a few things you can do to prepare yourself right now, including joining your school's drama club. Acting in plays will help you get comfortable in front of an audience. A lot of people are scared when they get onstage and see four thousand people in the stands. You don't want to look like a dead fish on your first day of work!

Most importantly, you should have a deep love for animals. Are you good with pets? Get a dog and try to teach it new tricks. Even better, try working with a cat, because they're harder to train. A bird, a goldfish, the type of animal doesn't really matter, it's being responsible for it that counts.

Don't be worried that you've never trained a dolphin before. New trainers get to watch the experienced trainers give their reinforcements and see the animals' reactions. Each dolphin is unique. They have their own individual personalities and specific likes and dislikes. New trainers learn by watching the dolphins interact with experienced trainers. Then they get to develop their own relationships with the dolphins, just as Renee and Mario did.

"Swimming with the dolphins isn't something that

could happen every day of my life," Renee said. "When I think of how beautiful and intelligent they are, I realize how important it is to tell others and help preserve the dolphins and other sea life."

Renee wanted to go to Dolphin Quest because she wants to help save the dolphins and other marine life. By taking *Name Your Adventure* viewers to this 350-million-gallon saltwater habitat where dolphins play and interact with humans every day, Renee helped us to understand as well how important it is to protect these incredible creatures.

Name *Your* Adventure

So there you have it—five educational and exciting environmental dreams-come-true for lucky viewers thanks to Mario, Jordan, and *Name Your Adventure*. If you'd like your adventure to come true, too, send a postcard to *Name Your Adventure*, P.O. Box 7304-506, North Hollywood, CA 91603. Tell us your name, address, grade, age, phone number, and adventure. You just might be the next lucky kid to have an exciting environmental adventure.

In the meantime, see what you can do for the environment and, as Mario says, "Keep it cool, and keep it safe!"